# Contents

## Acknowledgements

The first two editions of T*alking about Adoption
to your Adopted Child* were co-authored by Prue
Chennells and Marjorie Morrison. These editions, in
turn, were based on a previous book titled *Explaining
Adoption to your Adopted Child*, authored by
Prue Chennells.

This edition draws on the previous editions, but
contains new material and has been significantly
revised by Marjorie Morrison, former Child Placement
Consultant, BAAF Scotland, and takes account of any
significant legislative changes in England, Wales,
Scotland and Northern Ireland.

We would like to thank the following people for all
their suggestions and advice in the preparation of
this edition, including reading and commenting on
the script, rewriting sections or preparing new
material, and preparing text for production: Jennifer
Cousins, Jo Francis, Val Marwick, Brenda Reilly, Philly
Morrall, Christina Paulson-Ellis, Shaila Shah, Satnam
Singh, Stephanie Stone, Frances Nicholson and
Maureen Kinnell.

The quotations in this book are sourced in cases
where they have been extracted from a publication.
Unsourced quotes are as a result of personal
communications over the years.

Finally, this book could not have been written without
the wholehearted collaboration of many adopted
people and adoptive parents who generously shared
their experiences.

## Note about the author

Marjorie Morrison was a Child Placement Consultant with BAAF Scotland from 1981 to 2006, and has spent many years developing services to link children and families. This has extended to consultancy on planning, preparation of children for adoption, and also discussion through the BAAF telephone advice service with many adopters and adoptees post-adoption. Her first adoption experience was in the assessment of adopters for young children in Northern Ireland. Marjorie is also a co-author of *Making Good Assessments and Right from the Start*, both published by BAAF.

# Introduction: some basic principles

*I have friends who are adopted and all of us have felt differently at different times – it really mattered to know that whatever I felt was OK.*

## About this book

For newly approved adoptive parents, the excitement of passing that hurdle and thinking of the reality of a child joining their family is often allied with apprehension about all the responsibilities which will follow. Preparation groups and home studies will have explored many aspects of what lies ahead, highlighting a myriad of complexities. Equally, adoptive parents who have been caring for their children, perhaps for years, still have lots of questions about the best ways to approach tricky aspects at different stages.

There are a growing number of books and resources on the many facets of bringing up children who have joined a family through adoption. In the midst of them, parents are getting on with the day-to-day business of living, playing, working and talking with their children.

The purpose of this book is to highlight for you as prospective or existing adoptive parents some key aspects of helping your child understand her or his history and the circumstances that led to him or her joining your family. It is based on the experience and knowledge of many people who have been adopted, and that of adoptive parents. It does not aim to be the definitive text, but rather to encourage your own creativity and imagination and also to direct you to further resources and ideas. Your child's story may initially appear quite simple or have many complex areas to explore. He or she may have joined you as a baby, a toddler or when already of school age. Your adoption may have all happened locally or may have been from overseas. Your child may grow up expressing little interest in the past or be eager to trace birth relatives and have an endless flow of questions. Whatever your situation, we hope this book will help you.

We now also have a much more sophisticated understanding of how early adverse experiences can echo through childhood and into adulthood. Whether or not your child has direct memories of life before joining your adoptive family, inevitably talking about adoption will lead you into other areas. Whilst these may sometimes be distressing or painful, they can also be part of the healing process. Support in facing difficulties helps build your child's resilience and self-esteem and can often help to deepen your relationship with your child. At the end of each chapter, children and young people, adopters and others talk about their feelings and experiences.

This book does not set out to address the wider aspects of re-parenting children who have had a difficult start. Some suggestions are given at the end of the text for useful books on understanding child development and the impact of different events and experiences on this. Sometimes helping children explore the reasons for their adoption is central to their progress. At other times the emphasis might be on finding ways to manage behaviour which is causing them problems, and on day-to-day learning about family life in a positive way. The task is to weave these strands together without losing the sense of fun and joy in being a family together.

The focus of this book is on talking with **children**. Of course, it does not stop there. A key part of adolescence centres around developing a sense of who you are and where you fit. As adoptive parents you may be able to continue playing an important part in your child's quest – but we know that many adolescents look increasingly to their friends at this stage so the foundation needs to be well built during the earlier years. Many adults who were adopted continue to seek further knowledge and understanding of their origins at different periods throughout their lives. The last chapter looks at tracing birth relatives and the varied experiences of those who did not have contact with any birth family members during their childhood but met them later.

## Changing attitudes

It can come as quite a surprise now to talk to an adult whose adoption was kept a secret or who can recall the shock of finding out unexpectedly in an unplanned way. While the debate about whether to tell and how much to tell still continues around the growing methods of assisted reproduction, preparation for adoption is firmly and clearly rooted in a belief in openness and honesty. This position has been reached for various reasons.

For some people, the starting point was a commonsense pragmatic one. Their children would learn they were adopted at some point, so it was best that the knowledge and explanations came from their parents. Those earlier adopted adults who stumbled over evidence of their adoption at a later age often said things like, 'It wasn't so much that I was adopted that shocked me, more the fact that my mum and dad had been deceiving me for years'. Their parents, if they heard such comments, were likely to be saddened that what they saw as "protecting" their child was interpreted as deception.

Perhaps inevitably, once you move away from a climate of secrecy, the question of "rights" emerges. Most people would agree that everyone has the right to find out about their history and origins and many people, sooner or later, feel a deep need to know about it. Generally, children now may be more conscious of their rights and argue for them. At the same time, most families do not spend all their time debating rights. The important lesson that has been learnt by adoptive parents over the years is that the benefits of an open approach go well beyond pragmatic reasoning or arguments about rights. The strongest relationships are based on truth – adopters and adopted people have realised this for years and our legislation now recognises this too, for example, in relation to allowing adopted people to see their original birth certificate at the age of 16 (Scotland) or 18 (England, Wales and Northern Ireland). Practice now, however, goes well beyond this to encouraging and supporting a developing parent–child relationship built on honesty, trust, understanding, respect and compassion. Some of the strongest messages have come from adopted people themselves – adults of all ages who have sought information or reunion with birth families, and children, especially teenagers, who have met together and shared with each other their thoughts and feelings. There is now a huge amount of evidence about the extent to which adopted people wonder about their origins. A few may have had unhappy experiences of adoption. Many show great loyalty and caring for their adoptive families. They do not want to cause heartache for the parents who have brought them up. Some may be inhibited from talking to their adoptive parents because of their own sensitivity, others because they have picked up that this is a difficult area. This book is about thinking of positive, active ways that you as adopters can play your part. Saying this is not to imply that it will be straightforward.

Some adoptive parents, being honest with themselves, are very aware of the feelings this arouses in them. If you came to adoption because of childlessness, your preparation is likely to have included recognition that feelings about this, and the baby you had hoped you would have, can continue to emerge after your child joins your family. Adoptive parents may experience many other complex feelings:

- a strong need to "claim" this child;
- anger at what may have happened to your child;
- sadness for the birth parent and feelings of loss for everyone;
- apprehension about what lies ahead;
- protectiveness of your child and your family;
- high expectations of yourselves as parents and hopes for your child.

Learning about healthy relationships, developing a secure base from which to explore the wider world, establishing lasting values, and building self-esteem based on acceptance and "unconditional love" are all important features of a healthy family life. This child who joined your family through adoption may have gaps in his or her early history or difficult information to grapple with, which may be particularly pertinent in just these areas. You need to find convincing ways to assure your child of "unconditional love" while helping them understand why their birth parents are not looking after them. If your child still needs a lot of support in building self-esteem, how can you explain his or her background in a way which realistically builds confidence and self-respect? How do you deal with potential conflicts in values between yourselves and your child's birth family in a way that demonstrates a respectful approach, while being consistent with your own value base?

One of the early views of adoption was that it was an ideal solution for meeting the needs of both involuntarily childless adults and babies who could not be raised by their birth parents. This suggests a neat balancing of those needs. The combination of our more sophisticated understanding of adoption from adults who have been adopted and the nature of the children we are now placing has led to a shift in that balance. The emphasis is now clearly on what is best for the children. This is not about dismissing the needs of the adults, but it is based on a belief that it is in meeting the emotional and psychological needs of the child that adults will be able to create the healthy family experience they seek. In reaching that point there are likely to be times when doing what is best for the child will run counter to the wishes of the adults and will be uncomfortable.

## Some useful concepts

It is useful at the outset to have discussed some general guidelines about your approach and what makes sense to you. How you express yourself on a day-to-day basis will flow more easily if it is based on a clear idea in your head of what you hope to achieve over time. Thinking about this will have started during your preparation for adoption. The point when you are approved is a huge step forward towards the reality of adoptive parenthood, and the time to get ready to take on the responsibilities of this.

- Central to talking about adoption is talking about your child's birth family and why adoption was necessary. Before you start you need to be confident both about your status as adopters and also about handling the reality of the existence of the child's other "parents". This may be easy to say, but for many people it is a tough and emotionally demanding challenge when your original starting point was the desire to have "children of your own". Before you are linked with a particular child you need to be honest with yourselves that you have genuinely faced this. Then, when you hear about a child, you can move on from a general comfort with adoption to making sense of that child's individual history.

- At its simplest, adoption has two elements – the separation of the child from her or his first family, followed by their joining a new family. It is common to come across tensions between adults, with both prospective adopters and also the general public frequently focusing on the positive gains in creating this new family while others, especially social workers, appearing to emphasise all the losses in adoption. For the child who must make this move from being part of one family to another, it may be more helpful to think in terms of yin and yang and the need to balance these potential tensions in a healthy way over time. They are unlikely to be in balance all the time – at some stages the gains may predominate and at others the losses will come to the fore. You will need to hold on to the long-term perspective.

- Your child's understanding of their adoption will grow slowly and in stages. It may not be talked about all the time, but neither is there a point when it is "explained" and the task is complete.

- The most frequent response from adopted adults who are comfortable with their circumstances is that they "always knew". As your child is growing up, you will not know whether they will seek access to their adoption records as adults, or when that might happen. A useful target, therefore, is to think about all that might be there and aim to ensure that all the fundamental information you have is shared by that stage so there are no unnecessary shocks or surprises. Given that there are bound to be times when your child is not interested, is resistant, or has other preoccupations, this argues for starting early and giving yourself plenty of time to build up the picture.

- There is a difference between having information and making sense of it. The emphasis as your child grows up will shift from sharing factual information, to helping them consider the impact and implications for themselves. The nature of this task will vary depending on whether your child was very young when he or she joined you and is therefore dependent on you sharing their background information with them, or whether your child came with memories of experiences in their birth family and all the feelings these evoke.

- "Talking" about adoption is used here to indicate that positive thought needs to be given to how you communicate with your child about their circumstances. Adopted people who "always knew" may not recall being sat down and told, but clearly received a message that it was "OK to talk". Talking clearly implies a two-way communication where listening is just as important. Talking with younger children, in particular, also includes participation in other activities such as playing, drawing, acting and story-telling as well as direct conversation. Non-verbal communication can be as important as words, whether it is a hug when your child is upset by a thoughtless remark, or an acknowledgement of the cues that tell you your child is struggling with something they cannot put into words. Equally, if you told your child the basic fact of their adoption early but it has not come up again, you need to think about whether that lack of further discussion is neutral and demonstrates acceptance, or if your child is picking up that this is a difficult subject for you.

- Some adopters find it helpful to think about the distinction between talking of an "adopted child" and a child who joined your family through adoption – we are not talking about a different sort of child, but one with a different early history who became part of your family in a particular way. This approach avoids stereotypes or other people's assumptions about an adopted child, and also may be helpful for families which include children who joined it in different ways. Fortunately, this is becoming easier as society now recognises many different family structures. Your child will be going to school with children who have step- and half-brothers and sisters, and children who stay with one parent and visit the other. There are considerations that are special to adoption, particularly around the very planned way in which children move into a non-related family in which they subsequently legally belong. But there are also a number of aspects that are not unique to children who have been adopted.

- Identity is one of the central concepts in adoption. The strong need to know about their origins and roots felt by many adopted people has long been recognised. A healthy identity is both about knowing who you are and also feeling comfortable and confident about that. Some aspects such as gender and ethnicity are "given" and are part of our genetic inheritance. How positive your child feels about those aspects is influenced by his or her upbringing. Your child's potential to develop certain abilities and aptitudes may come from birth parents but be nurtured in your family. There are clear links between self-esteem and a well-established identity. Hopefully, you will be able to help your child draw together her or his knowledge of birth family, genetic factors and early history alongside the place of adoption in his or her life. This, together with all his or her formative experiences and relationships in your family, will help form a rounded picture. At the end of the day, you are helping your child find the answer for himself or herself to the question, 'Who am I?' and that includes **all** aspects of his or her life. In practice she or he may have moved from one family into another – but your child's identity will incorporate both.

- Some adopters find it helps to think of their child's birth family as being like an extension of the adoptive family; it is not a conflict between "our" or "your" child, but an understanding of a joint concern for the wellbeing of "their" child, with full recognition of the importance of both the birth and adoptive parents. This is about thinking of the birth parents as having a place on your mental "map" of your child's network. Your child's individual circumstances will indicate whether it would be helpful for the birth parents to play a direct part in your child's life at any particular point.

For some children, valuing their occasional face-to-face contact with birth family members may be an essential element in choosing your family to adopt them. For others, any thought of contact may only arise when they become adults.

- One of the most common hopes expressed by parents for their children is that they will be happy. One of the anticipated joys of adoption is of offering children happy childhood experiences, especially if they have had few good times in the past and far too many bad experiences. It is a natural response to want to leave the past behind. What we have learnt from adopted adults is that life is not that simple. Some adopted adults have expended emotional energy over many years in trying to make sense of their past history. For many of these adults, the legacy of unresolved issues from early childhood has interfered with their ability to move on with their lives. There are many factors that can affect happiness in the long run; some, like personality, life events or luck evolve or happen as life goes on. Effective parents also think about ways they can bring up their children to increase their chances of having a fulfilling future. Generally, this includes aspects like offering them opportunities to benefit from education; developing healthy lifestyles; exploring their aptitudes and interests; learning about relationships and social skills; and building a supportive network of family and friends. Inevitably, there are times when families hit difficult periods. At these times, adults need to find the right balance between protecting their children and helping them learn how to cope with issues and perhaps emerge stronger. For adoptive families, the challenges may come along with the child and their earlier experiences. What adopters can do to increase their child's chance of a positive future is to give them the skills and strategies to manage the ups and downs of life. This means not evading the difficult aspects of their child's background but thinking actively over time about building strength and competence in handling their history.

No matter what route you took to becoming an adoptive parent, we hope you will find some useful ideas in this book. We would encourage you to use the growing opportunities now available to link with other adoptive parents and also to use established adoption support services. These must now be provided in the UK for anyone who wishes advice or counselling in relation to adoption. Services are developing all the time, not just for when you have problems, but also to support you in doing the best for your child.

## Thoughts and feelings

*I think growing up with that openness and recognition that I was my own person who would do my own thing helped me be closer to my adoptive parents.*

*I always knew. It was really important that the information I got when I was young was honest and truthful. After about 11, it was as though I started thinking more like an adult.*

---

*I've traced my birth mum now. I don't think I had any "fantasy family" in my mind but I still don't fully understand all the reasons why I was adopted. There were no big dramatic stories.*

---

*Having photographs mattered. They are tangible, something to hold on to that is special and personal to me.*

---

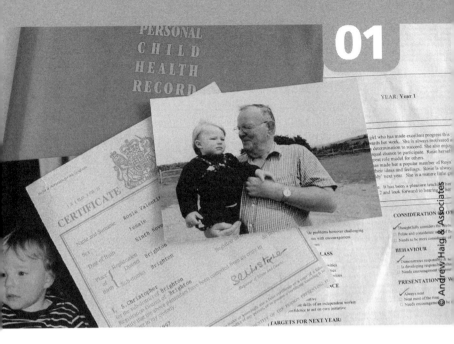

# 01

# Starting to talk about adoption

*I usually chose the time when she was wrapped in her towel and lying on the mat after her bath – a nice secure time. Obviously it wasn't every bath time but as she learned to talk she would ask me at this particular time to tell her about my visits to the foster home to see her and 'What did we all say?' She, like many children, likes repetition – it seems to give security – and at first it was like another fairy tale for her. Now it's a reality, and a pleasant one.*

Although far fewer babies are placed for adoption nowadays, there are thousands and thousands of adopted children and adults in the UK. Families in general vary considerably, with many children experiencing the separation or divorce of parents, forming new relationships with step-parents or spending at least part of their childhood with a single parent. We know all these areas are discussed much more openly now than in the past, including directly with the children concerned. Adoption is also talked about more openly now, both within families and in the wider community, including the media. This, however, does not automatically make it easier for adoptive parents to feel comfortable in approaching discussion of something which is so close to the heart of their family life.

## The first step

Adoptive parents often worry about "getting it right". As adults, we may be very aware of all the complex information we have and the amount we may need to share. This first step, however, is about establishing basic communication about adoption and letting your child know it is something that can be talked about. This applies whether your child joined you soon after birth and is relying on you to introduce the subject, or came at a later stage, having done some life story work but needing to find out how you, as his or her new adoptive parents, will respond.

The first step is about opening the door to an important area of your child's life. Children vary tremendously in how they explore things. Some may plunge in with lots of questions for a while, then move on to something else. Others are more cautious and may only want to know very little, before returning to more familiar preoccupations. Many children do not share their concerns through words, either because of their age or because saying some things is too scary. Some children may be aware, or sense, dark corners that will need to be explored slowly and tentatively with your support. Ultimately, a realistic idea of what is there is healthier than undefined fears or fantasies. Older children may be able to gain confidence through being able to share their memories with you and knowing you will listen carefully. They may also wish to keep certain doors closed for a period.

For adults, it can help to think about or rehearse a few simple words to get started – try saying the words in your head to see what comes easily and if there are bits you stumble over. It may help to identify a useful "trigger" event, when the topic could be introduced naturally – perhaps a visit to a former foster home or a celebration of the granting of the adoption order. You may need to consciously create an opening or prompt an older child who can equally feel awkward or uncomfortable about bringing the subject up, and be less equipped to find the right words. Early thinking and planning will help you feel more in control. If you are adopting as partners, one person may feel more confident in taking the lead.

If you convey a positive sense of adoption to your child and he or she grows up knowing that you are willing to talk about their reality, that firm base will stand them in good stead as years go by. Whatever your child's age, warmth and affection are very important ingredients in sharing information. Body language matters at least as much as the actual words used. Some people show their feelings more readily than others and, equally, your child will be picking up the emotional climate in your family. What matters is that the child does not feel overwhelmed by feelings she or he does not understand or becomes reluctant to bring the topic up again. One of the initial things that you will be picking up from your child is his or her level of comfort with physical affection and how best to offer reassurance. It also helps to have established some family routines that you can use to confirm the security of their place with you.

## If your child was placed as a baby

If you adopted your child when he or she was very young, you can start talking at an early age. The fact that your child is adopted will be just another fact to be taken in along with all the other information being learned. Your child will not understand what adoption means, but will become familiar with the term as something you are positive about and that is an open subject between you. But do not feel that you have to stress adoption all the time. If you keep dwelling on the fact that adoption is special and different you may find your child expects special treatment! A very few simple facts are enough to set the foundation that your child is adopted and had other "first" parents before coming to live with you. Some people use commercially available books as bedtime stories to introduce the idea; others prefer to start making the child's own personal book themselves, building on early details of their child's life, and any "first" photographs they might have. Alongside these planned approaches you can also be on the lookout for opportunities to make spontaneous comments. Popular "soaps" may bring up questions or a child's interest in what happened to an abandoned or lost baby animal in a nature programme can be used to advantage. There are also specific programmes about adoption on TV at intervals. Even if your child does not understand much, they will pick up your interest. Much of the communication with young children does not happen in a formal way but rather through chatting together while playing or doing normal household activities together. Often these are brief exchanges that keep adoption on the agenda without making it a heavy issue. They will help you monitor when your child needs a bit more information, or has got some of the facts mixed up.

## WHAT TO CALL THE BIRTH PARENTS

We have used the term "birth parent" to describe the child's biological parent. What term you use is up to you: "first parent" is one possibility, and can also be used to describe divorced parents of your children's friends, thus showing that plenty of other children have "first" mums and dads. Other adopters have pointed out that they avoided "new" mummy and daddy for themselves as it sounded like a replacement and they wanted all parties to have their place and be valued. For very young children, "tummy mummy" sums it up very well. Some adopters prefer to use first names: 'Well, you grew in Elizabeth's tummy and then you came to mummy and daddy.' For obvious reasons, the term "real parent", to describe the birth parent, is not a good choice as it may make you appear less "real". The term "natural parent" has similar disadvantages. As well as a general term you also need to be sure that your child can distinguish who she or he is talking about – and that you have this clear as well. You may need, for example, to talk about "mummy Jean" or "daddy John", who was your child's birth mum or dad.

## If your child joined you as a toddler

Toddlers are too young to understand what adoption means or to have enough language ability to tell you what they are thinking or feeling. However, the placement of a toddler always needs careful planning as they are certainly aware of being moved. Toddlers can find this a very difficult and distressing time and need a lot of help and support from both the foster carers they have been with, and their new adoptive parents. Part of this often involves finding very concrete ways to help them understand that the adoptive family is where they will be staying and establishing their long-term security.

Some toddlers may have moved a number of times and words like "forever" will not make sense without lots of thought about how they can be helped to understand they will not be moving again. This is where actions and words need to go hand-in-hand. Paying attention to the messages conveyed to pre-school children in practical ways as they move into your family will start you on the right path. Some foster carers are particularly skilful at passing on to new adopters information that is especially important to a child in front of them. This provides a really good opening and pointers to build on. Photographs of the introduction period, and, in some instances, visits back to the foster carers can be natural prompts for confirming the information given and finding out if the child needs to ask any more questions. Some foster carers are particularly imaginative with toddlers and you may be able to build on this. One foster carer with a two-year-old, for example, used large cut-out footprints laid out as a path and posters of houses to play games of going from one place to another. There are all sorts of ways that this could be extended both to bring in the added step of the first move from the birth parents and to use other toys and props to play out remaining in the adoptive family – the finishing point of the "game". There are also a growing number of children's books which can help in opening up discussion both about adoption and what life is like for children in difficult circumstances (see Useful Books).

With both babies and toddlers, it may feel as though you are starting from scratch if they are at the early stages of language development and you are not aware of particular conscious memories that they have. One of the challenges in adoption work has been hearing about some adults placed as very young children who appear to have a vulnerability about their adoption even though they have had a very secure childhood in their adoptive home. There are no neat formulae to explain everything about this and of course many adopted adults are at ease with their adoption history. There is, however, more information available now about the importance of early brain development in children and just how much is being absorbed and retained during the pre-verbal stages. Just think about the changes between a newborn baby and a one-year-old. They have learnt a tremendous amount about the world and their place within it, not through verbal explanations but in absorbing information through all their senses, dependent on their environment and interaction with the adults caring for them. Sometimes echoes of intense feelings from the past may be triggered by something in their current environment which they cannot explain but has somehow tapped into a past memory stored in the brain.

Opportunities for developing their view of their world may emerge from watching your child play and thinking about when and how it might help to join in. If your child, for example, keeps playing very

Here is an illustration from the chapter titled 'Substance misuse, attachment disorganisation and adoptive families', by Caroline Archer, in *Children Exposed to Parental Substance Misuse* (Philips (ed), 2004).

Sian,18, is the mother of Karl.

'Karl, born prematurely, is five months old...He is lying on the floor surrounded by discarded drinks containers, decaying food, soiled nappies and cigarette ends. The threadbare carpet is stained, the room is chilly. Sian is lying on the bed listening to loud music, oblivious to Karl's whimpering. Emotionally, Sian is unable to provide Karl with the consistency of nurturing care he needs...Instead, he frequently experiences unpredictability and powerlessness...This reinforces Karl's feelings of terror and neglect. His burgeoning, internal working models (Bowlby, 1973, 1988), or inner "road maps" (Archer and Burnell, 2003) formed from real-world experiences, reinforce his perceptions that he is worthless, helpless and abandoned.'

The further exploration in this chapter about the strength of the sensory experiences of such young children vividly shows what a child will be learning about the world before she or he has any language to explain it.

**References**
Archer C and Burnell A (eds) *Trauma, Attachment and Family Permanence*, London: Jessica Kingsley Publishers

Bowlby J (1973) *Separation: Anxiety and Anger*, London: Hogarth Press

Bowlby J (1988) *A Secure Base*, London: Routledge

aggressively with dolls or soft toys you might want to pick the moment to act as rescuer and "comfort" the toy. This is about offering other alternatives through play rather than telling a child not to do something. You may well have at the back of your mind some information about what your child could have experienced at an earlier stage. Demonstrating to your child what dependent infants – and teddies! – need is one aspect of giving them both the experiences and the language of what caring parents do. This may well be part of the explanation of why they could not stay with their birth parents. Play or symbolic actions may need to come first – think, for example, how parents might deal with nightmares or monsters under the bed! It helps to be conscious of the added significance of seemingly ordinary play for children who have missed out on good early experiences and in particular to give them the words to understand when you explain their story.

Often the first stage is talking about **what** happened to your child in the past, perhaps in very concrete terms, and as time goes on you will need the language to explain **why** their birth parents could not manage to care for them.

In your preparation for adoption you will have learnt about the importance of attachments and the centrality of this in the first weeks and months of life. Equally, if you observe babies you will see how they express their feelings and how dependent they are on how their primary carers respond – whether they are happy, sad, uncomfortable or distressed. Of course, all babies will have times when they are separated from their mothers for brief periods and show reactions to this. Normally, their mother comes back and they learn to manage such day-to-day events. For all adopted children, the person they first got to know while in the womb left and did not return. Skilled temporary foster carers are very good at finding ways to soothe such babies but somewhere within their experience these children have had the feeling of being "abandoned" and, especially at times of change, those feelings may return. As adopters, you will need to find the best ways to support your child if times like starting nursery or school or going into hospital leave them feeling vulnerable. This may involve extra hugs, allowing space for them to revert to younger behaviour, or providing small photographs of yourselves or objects for a child to tuck into a pocket and take with them.

In thinking of your child's adoption story, it may also help to find simple words to acknowledge how he or she might have felt as a baby and what they can do now if they are feeling bereft or lost. This is about building into the story over time an understanding of feelings and how your child can avoid being overwhelmed by these. In fact, this is what all parents start to do with very young children as they recognise and respond to their babies when they cannot offer verbal explanations. Sometimes this leads to stories that are shared with children later – many people can recall family stories about themselves even if they are not sure that they have their own independent memory of the event. This could include discovering just the right blanket or toy to help your child feel better – and any adventures when it was lost! You may feel sad that you were not there when your young child needed a cuddle from a familiar person, but in the long run it is better to include an understanding of how an experience might have felt from the child's perspective rather than avoid or deny how it might have been.

To help with this, you might like to keep a diary of your observations of your child in the early stages of joining your family. Noting how they react to different sounds or normal day-to-day activities alongside information from social workers and former carers can provide lots of clues about what your child may have felt at times before he or she came to your family. Beginning to talk about this with your child is likely to come later but having some detailed information to look back at can guide you in thinking what may be important to acknowledge to help your child's emotional development.

What is common to children of all ages who are placed for adoption is that after all the thinking, planning and learning, suddenly adoptive parents are confronted with the reality of meeting this new person who is intended to be their son or daughter. With newborn babies we talk of the "dance of attunement" and its role in forming attachments. In a different way this needs to happen with adoptive parents too. This includes learning when your child needs reassurance, recognition of confused or unhappy feelings or when they need a boost of confidence and direction towards the strengths they can build on for their future. There are obvious connections here to the specific task of helping children understand about all the aspects of their adoption.

## Introducing adoption to older children

Adoption is not just about babies and toddlers: nowadays, children who have reached school age are also adopted. For these children, learning that there are no longer plans for them to return to their birth parents, and then being introduced to the idea of going to live with adoptive parents, normally happens in their foster home. So, the initial talk about adoption is done by the foster carer and/or your child's social worker. It is helpful to know exactly what was said, so that you can build on familiar words and ideas.

---

'He [social worker] had to explain it to me a couple of times and then I had my queries…it took me quite a while. And I kept asking questions all over again and he answered them.'

'I wasn't quite sure what adoption actually meant, but I knew it was a place where I would stay and be looked after.'

'I was quite surprised actually…Any child would be surprised if they knew their parents were going to give you to someone else. Any child would be surprised.'

'In a little dream thinking…you were never gonna move on and the process was a bit slow. But on the other hand it kinda went quick if you didn't think about it a lot…A bit of a dream. Adrift.'

Quotes from children on starting the adoption process
From *Adopted Children Speaking* (Thomas and Beckford, 1999)

---

While many children are relieved at being offered the security of adoption or are desperate to be claimed, the possibility of this change can bring conflicting feelings about parents to the surface. For older children, at least, part of starting to talk about adoption relates to information within their conscious memory.

It is often important in introducing adoption and finding a language to talk about both birth parents and adoptive parenting not to put the child into the position of "choosing". Use of visual portrayals like the three circles for birth parent, legal parent and parenting parent can help older children see that their birth parents still have a place in their lives, even if legal responsibility for them changes.

## Aspects of parenting

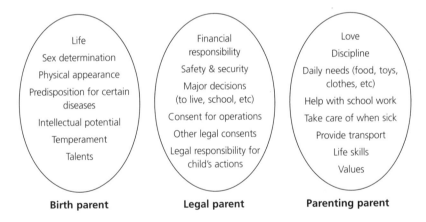

The above figure is taken from *A Child's Journey through Placement* by Vera Fahlberg (BAAF, 1994)

As adopters, try imagining the content of the two circles in the diagram above entitled *Legal parent* and *Parenting parent* written on paper figures. Now think how often this is all fragmented for children who eventually enter adoptive families. Social workers and courts become involved in all sorts of decisions usually made by parents and many children are cared for by various family members or friends and then by different temporary foster carers while planning goes on around them. The lives of these children may have been literally torn apart just as you can rip up those paper figures. In assuming responsibility for one of these children, adoptive families are gathering together their fractured lives. This is a tremendously positive and important task and it is vital to hold on to this fact if you are feeling at a low ebb. The reality alongside this is that the one "aspect" you cannot take on is being the birth parent. Ultimately, to become a whole person, the child has to put all these aspects in perspective. Your responsibility is to help your child achieve that. Of course it will be complex, sometimes it will be emotionally challenging and it will need to be managed in relation to the child's different ages and stages. Keeping in mind the three aspects of parenting from the start can help you in developing a consistent explanation and language. At the same time, hopefully it will enable you to feel confident about the value of your parenting role while accepting the place of the child's birth family. (See also *What is a parent?* in Chapter 10.)

With older children, such ideas may already have been introduced by social workers and foster carers to help prepare children to move to a permanent family. The timing of any discussion of adoption with a child in foster care is very important as it can raise such high hopes and expectations. This may have prompted various questions and anxieties, especially if some level of contact with birth family members is ongoing. Foster carers try to work very closely with children's social workers firstly to try and avoid a situation where children lose confidence or self-esteem if an adoptive family is not found quickly, and secondly, to try to be sure that everyone understands each child's particular concerns at the point when they will be meeting a new family.

For new adoptive parents, meeting a well-prepared older child can be quite overwhelming, particularly if the child immediately "claims" you! If you are in that position, as well as finding out all about the child's background, it is important to know just what they have been told and discuss what might come up – even during introductions.

Just as we know it is important for foster carers to give children "permission" to move into your family, so too it helps if you can form a clear link between how they have been preparing the child and what you can pick up and build on in the early stages of placement. In the research carried out by Caroline Thomas and Verna Beckford, titled *Adopted Children Speaking* (1999), the authors talked to 41 children between the ages of eight and 15 who had been adopted at the age of five or older. They found the early part of the process the most difficult stage. The children found it hard to remember the beginning steps; they had only vague memories of being introduced to the idea and how they were prepared varied considerably. As an interesting contrast, when a review of adoption services was underway in Scotland, a small piece of research was commissioned seeking the views of older children who had remained in the care system long term. Most were teenagers, some in foster care and some in residential care. Apart from the fact that only one had a direct memory of adoption being raised as an option, virtually all the young people had by this later stage developed a clear idea of what adoption meant and had their own perceptions about whether it would have been a benefit for them or not. This would suggest that while your children are growing up, even if you do not talk much about it with them, their views will be developing in the light of outside influences.

In coming into the picture as a new adoptive parent, it is wise not to assume that your child has understood all that she or he has been told so far. It is also important that you establish your willingness to share their story with them early on. It may not be the start of your child talking about adoption, but it is the beginning of **your** communication with him or her.

One of the aspects older children recall in learning about their
adoption is that it is a legal process – a court makes a decision. It
takes sensitivity to realise when it is right for everyone to proceed
with the necessary steps to complete the legal adoption. This is an
important and significant step in a growing relationship and the
court will also take into account your child's views and wishes
depending on his or her age and understanding. In Scotland,
children aged 12 or over need to sign their own agreement to their
adoption. Introducing the decision to adopt includes steps that are
very clear and visible to the child such as the visit of the court
appointed Children's Guardian, in Scotland the curator *ad litem*. This
can precipitate fresh talk about thoughts and feelings that may have
lain dormant or are linked to a new phase in your child's
development. While many welcome this step as confirmation of
their security in their adoptive family, for others it may cause a
resurgence of ambivalent feelings about their past and birth family.
This may be a natural and understandable "wobble" but obviously
causes anxiety about the timing. This is when you need to call on
your social worker and talk through everyone's concerns while
keeping the long-term aims of the adoption in mind.

Most families mark and celebrate the granting of the order in some
way, and may continue to celebrate the anniversary. The
confirmation that you are now legally a family is an important
staging post in your child's understanding of adoption. Thinking
each year of revisiting that is a useful way of reviewing whether and
how your child's understanding and knowledge are developing,
including whether she or he is entering a more complex and
sensitive stage. Any such celebration is, of course, about confirmimg
your child's place in your family. You might like to think about ways
near this time – or other significant dates – to check if your child
also has thoughts about the absent birth family. This may be by
looking again at any photographs of birth family members, finding a
place for a memento or gift from your child's earlier life or perhaps
developing a family ritual like lighting a particular candle that
represents people from the child's first family who matter to her or
him. This should not feel as though you are forcing such thoughts
to the fore or that you have to include some reminder of the past in

events that are about your family now. It is more about finding quiet, non-confrontational ways of signalling that you have not forgotten, that you accept that your child might be having other thoughts and it is OK if they want to talk about them.

## Thoughts and feelings

*I was surprised at how little our daughter wanted to know about the more difficult "whys" and "wherefores" when she first started asking questions aged about five. I was on the brink of delivering a carefully scripted hour's lecture in response to her question, 'Why couldn't Mary [her birth mother] look after me?' She was quite happy with a one-liner! It was several years before she wanted to know the details.*

# 02

# What information do you need?

*It's essential to be absolutely honest. You mustn't tell them anything that isn't true or leave out anything important. By the time our kids are grown up, they will probably be able to see their own social services records, and if they find out that we've been in any way untruthful they'll never trust us again.*

In thinking about the information you need, you should bear in mind the purpose of this. Early research, such as *In Search of Origins* (Triseliotis, 1973), which was undertaken when many babies were placed because of the social stigma of single parenthood, emphasised the strong need of adopted people for details of birth parents as part of understanding their identity. Now there is equal emphasis on having the kind of information that answers the question, 'Why was I adopted?' – and all that is linked to that.

## Asking questions

Adoption agencies in the UK are required by law to give you, the adoptive parent, written information about your child's background. When you first hear about a child it is easy to get caught up in finding out all the details of what she or he is like. In addition, nowadays, many of the young children placed have additional concerns surrounding their development, which you need to examine. In the midst of all this, including considering whether this is a child you could parent, it is easy to view the whole range of details about the child's birth family as an area for future exploration when your family is more settled. This is where thinking long term and being alert to all the potential needs of the child in the years ahead will pay off. While many details will be recorded in various reports, often it adds a lot to be able to talk to those who already know both the child and her or his parents well. Your child is likely to welcome your personal attention to this material on their behalf. This is when it is freshest and you will also pick up on feelings that will help your own understanding.

Find out as much as you can about your child's birth parents – their family history, their jobs and interests, their physical characteristics and health, significant family members and family folklore. Knowledge about things like height and build will come in useful the day your child asks questions like: 'How come I'm so tall/short/fat/thin?' And you really need medical information to be able to answer questions like: 'Any family history of asthma/eczema/heart disease?' Your doctor may have your child's medical records but not the details of other family members. Your child may turn out to be particularly keen on music, or sport, or mathematics, and it would be useful to be able to say, 'Well, your mother/father was a musician/dancer/footballer/engineer, etc'. Anything you can find out will be valuable, but you may find you have to keep asking. The social workers who have worked with your child's birth parent(s) could have information that may not seem important to them but could be fascinating for your child.

However, no list of questions can be complete. For example, adopters, when asked, can be very satisfied with all the medical information they receive – yet still be prompted to come back with fresh questions springing from media publicity about new medical advances indicating predispositions to certain conditions in biological families. So perhaps the most important piece of information is about ways to try to find out answers to new questions in the future and what your agency can offer in this respect.

There will, sadly, be some children for whom little or no information will be available. This is particularly so for the small number of children abandoned in this country and also for some children placed through intercountry adoption. It is still important to ensure that you have every possible detail about how your child became known to those who are now placing her or him for adoption and that you establish ways for any information that emerges in the future to reach you. You may or may not be lucky in unearthing at least some information for your child but it is also important that in the years ahead they know that you did all you could at the time and that you understood how it could feel if all you could say when your child asked was 'Sorry, I don't know'. Newspaper reports often include details of what babies were wearing or wrapped in as part of the appeal for information about the birth mother. Hopefully you will also receive any items left with your child. There is usually also a story about how a name was chosen for an abandoned baby. The place where they were found is frequently very significant, especially if it shows that the mother was anxious that her child would be found easily and was protected from the weather.

At the time your child joins your family, his or her medical records will be transferred to your GP from the GP with whom she or he was registered in the foster home. This record may be quite extensive on older children or children who have medical or developmental issues, or a known disability or impairment. The community paediatric service may also have extensive records and as more authorities have nurses for looked after children, increasing efforts are being made to ensure that gaps in medical information are filled as far as possible. If your child came from overseas, you may have an intercountry medical report (Form ICA), and BAAF has produced a Practice Note for parents and health professionals on the health screening of children adopted from abroad (2004). Obtaining medical information about your child's birth family is more complex because of confidentiality, but where co-operation and consent are available, at least a partial family medical history may be available. Until recently it was practice to complete a pre-adoption medical when the plan for adoption was made. This has now shifted to seeking full information on a child's health soon after they enter the care system. This enables the local authority to offer the child the sort of medical support you would expect of a parent. Medical advisers often provide written information to interpret and expand the medical examination. They may be available to talk to you, or this information may be provided in a helpful form for you to retain. All the key information from the various medical services your child may have attended before joining you should be in the GP's records. Practice can vary in minor ways, so you might like to clarify local arrangements with your agency.

It is crucial that you write down anything you discover. You might think you will remember, but you might not need some of this information for 10 or 15 years and your memory may not be so good then! When you do need it, you will find that having all the details written down will be invaluable. And obviously you will need to keep it all in a safe place.

If you adopted your child years ago and are missing lots of information, it is still worth getting back in touch with the adoption agency to try and find out more. Social workers, foster carers and children's home staff may all remember various things and have useful facts to give you. Keeping in touch with them occasionally is a good idea and makes it easier to get further information later on. You should also think about the different sorts of written information that would be helpful.

---

## SOME QUESTIONS YOU MIGHT ASK:

- What day was she or he born and at what time?
- Was it an easy or difficult birth?
- How long did she or he stay with the birth mother?
- Where did she or he go then? (find out as much detail as possible, according to the child's age)
- When did she or he have their first tooth, take their first steps, say their first words, etc?
- Why did they choose that particular name for the baby?
- Does she or he have any brothers or sisters – full, half or step?
- Where are they now?
- Where did the birth parents' families come from?
- Where were they both living when she or he was born?
- How old was the birth mother? And father?
- What did they look like?
- What did they wish for her or him?
- What did other family members know or think about the birth of the child?
- How would the birth mother and father describe their own families and what would they like the child to know?
- Do they have certain views or values that they would wish to share?
- What were their likes and dislikes?
- What were their hobbies and skills?
- Where did they work? What is their view on jobs they have done?
- What sort of schools did they go to?

Some of these questions could be asked of the birth parents if you have the opportunity to meet them.

You will be able to think of other questions. Try writing a list for yourself to tick off as you get answers.

## Meeting birth parents

Such meetings have been regularly offered to relinquishing birth parents for some years. Some birth parents of older children who have lost their children through a court process can also benefit from meeting their child's adoptive parents when the time is right. Any such meetings with birth family members are usually well planned, organised and supported. Sometimes the information about why a child is not safe in the care of a certain birth parent make adopters very wary about meeting them. In fact, most birth parents come across first and foremost as sad or vulnerable people. Seeing the real person may dispel myths for you and make it easier later to talk with your child about any unpalatable facts with some understanding of their birth parents' failures. In a few instances there may be good reasons why a meeting should not take place, or it may hold dangers. It is particularly important then that you are very confident about your ability to share difficult information and give realistic guidance about the wisdom of tracing in the future without overwhelming a child with fears about their birth family.

Despite being emotionally demanding for everyone, most adoptive parents find the long-term value of such meetings merits the time invested in them. That personal connection helps many adopters talk to their children about their birth parents with greater feeling. For your child, a photograph of such a meeting can convey a really strong message of permission to settle in their adoptive family. Their birth parents knew who would be adopting their child and acknowledged the adoption plan, whether or not they could bring themselves to sign their legal agreement. If this is something that still lies ahead for you, you might like to prepare some questions to give the meeting a focus.

Asking birth parents if there was a story around their choice of name for the child, for example, gives you more details to share with your child later and also conveys respect and recognition to the birth parent. If the initial face-to-face meeting is being followed by an arrangement for exchange of information, this can help start it off on a sound footing. Birth parents appreciate knowing that the child will hear about them as they are growing up and that you, as the adoptive parents, are interested in knowing such details to share. Birth parents may find it upsetting to talk too much about the reasons behind the adoption plan for their child but may be able to confirm what might have been written in a letter or has been explained by the social worker.

It can help some birth parents to include other members of their family in such meetings or it may be more realistic to meet helpful relatives. Whatever is suggested, you need to focus on what will help you answer questions in the future. A roomful of people might tell you a lot about family dynamics, but also leave you confused!

Some adopters say honestly that their apprehension about meeting birth parents is the fact that this makes them "real". This, of course, is one of the main purposes. It is worth reflecting on your reactions if this affects you. If you still have times when you feel upset thinking that your child had other parents before you, it is best to acknowledge that and find ways to ensure that this does not become a barrier in meeting your child's needs. On the other hand, you may be the sort of person who readily tunes in with the feelings of others and is very sensitive to the position of the birth parent. This will be a great help in talking compassionately to your child, but you need to be sure that you fully understand why the adoption is in your child's best interests. The time to talk through any doubts or ambivalence is now, not in the future with your child.

## Information to keep

You may have information aimed at your "adult" understanding and also something written for your child. You need to discuss with your social worker at what age it is appropriate to share this. This is what is sometimes called a "later life letter". It should not contain any surprises for you or your child, so you need to be aware of what is in it and have shared the information over the preceding years. For some children, these letters hold an emotional significance as a direct link back to the person who helped their birth parent plan for their future. If the birth mother has written a letter, or is prepared to do so, again it helps to know how it is written, at what age it could helpfully be shared with your child, and what level of understanding your child would need in order to make best use of the information. More importantly, you will need to be aware of the possible impact on your child of holding a letter written by their birth parent rather than a report of the facts. Some birth parents may have made a tape either on their own initiative or with encouragement from their agency. The actual voice of the birth parent is likely to be particularly powerful. Viewing or listening to such material with your child conveys a strong message of acceptance. Showing some emotion at such times is natural and your child is likely to appreciate your understanding and some shared sadness as long as it is accompanied by a supportive hug. Obviously you will need to keep items like this safe – there may well be copies in your child's adoption record that they can see when they are older, but these will not be the same as the originals.

## MATERIAL YOU WILL FIND USEFUL

- Written information about your child (required by law and supplied by adoption agency).
- Photographs of your child as a baby, a toddler, etc.
- Photographs of your child's birth family.
- Any other documents or mementos of your child's birth family, such as a letter from the birth parent, or a video tape.
- Any updating information, e.g. through a Post Box.
- A life story book about your child if one has been prepared.

- A family tree.
- Gifts from the birth family.
- Items from your child's earlier weeks, months or years with knowledge of their significance. Some foster carers keep locks of hair or first teeth!

---

As many children nowadays are placed for adoption past babyhood, you will, of course, need to know as much as possible about what has happened to your child since birth. It is important not to be rushed into absorbing this information and to take your time to understand what it might mean for your child.

Often, reports are written for social work meetings, adoption panels, or for the courts and might not tell you all you need to know as adoptive parents. You should also be able to meet key people who have been involved in caring for your child.

## Understanding the reasons for adoption

For your child, the key question is likely to be, 'Why was I adopted?' The simple answer, 'Your birth parent(s) could not look after you, and I (we) wanted a child very much, so you came to live with us,' will do for a start. But why the birth parent(s) could not manage will need explaining in more detail as the child gets older. Sometimes the initially less problematic backgrounds can be tricky in this respect. Now that so many single parents keep their children, those who appear capable people but choose to place their child for adoption can be harder for the child to understand. Some children are particularly sensitive to the thought of rejection, that they were not wanted, or that somehow if their birth parent was "OK" then he or she must have been a "bad" child.

Having a real understanding and "feel" for the birth parents will help you in making sense of their decisions and actions for your child. Some women may continue to experience the shame of single parenthood within some cultural and religious groups in the UK. Adoptive parents who share their child's ethnicity or religious background will have a real knowledge of the pressures on a birth parent, even if their individual views are a little different.

At the time you are linked with a child, you are likely to have plenty of questions about her or his needs. You will also find out about the reasons for the adoption plan. There is so much to absorb, and then you are plunged into the day-to-day integration of this child into your family. It is often only much later that you realise the importance of knowing about all the influences – both personal and cultural – on your child's birth parents that led to the adoption plan. This is particularly relevant if you do not share your child's original background and heritage, and need to find other ways to fill the gaps for your child beyond generalised statements. There are similar issues for intercountry adopters. If you have a live ongoing link with a particular country – for example, if you originally came from there or have lived and worked there – you will understand how that society works and the impact of traditions and values on individuals, especially pregnant women. Your child will be growing up surrounded by family, friends and probably a local community that may be based on different values and attitudes from those surrounding their birth parents. They will need you to help them make the leap of understanding and learn to respect other people's beliefs and attitudes.

It is worth thinking about the reports and records your child may see twenty or more years later. Do they put his or her individual circumstances in the wider social context? If your child is from another country, do you have sensible, balanced material about the reality of life there when your child was born? If you visit in twenty years' time, social attitudes may have changed considerably. In some countries such as China it is possible, for example, to buy local papers in English. When you visit, look out for these as they may be useful to keep for your child's future understanding – especially if they include articles on social issues of the time. Many intercountry adopters do a lot of research before embarking on that route, including finding out about the needs and requirements of different countries. These too will change over time. Both the official goverment website and the Intercountry Adoption Centre website (www.icacentre.org.uk) offer information about many individual countries. It is well worth keeping a copy of what you found out when you started adopting as it will help your child understand both the view of their country of origin when they were born and also what influenced you.

---

'It doesn't really matter what other people think. I know who I am...I can say proudly that I'm half Scottish and half Indian and that my nationality is British and Australian and that I was raised by white, English parents...It always makes for an interesting conversation when someone asks me where I'm from and I now have the choice as to how much I wish to disclose.'

From 'Tattie 'n' chapatti', by Jenny Mohindra, a transracially adopted person, in *In Search of Belonging*, (Harris, 2006)

---

There are, of course, many personal reasons why parents request adoption for their children. It may be relatively easy to put yourself into the shoes of a young mother with very little support who is struggling to care for herself, never mind look after a young baby. You may struggle more to understand other birth parents, but doing this early on will help you later in talking to your child. You may also be able to call on particular experiences from your own background that take on significance for you when you hear about a child. As well as helping your understanding, this will prepare you for feelings that might emerge later. If you have personal experience of discrimination or racism, you may be able to use this positively to understand a birth parent who is convinced her family will not accept or welcome this particular child because of his or her parentage. If you have chosen to adopt a child with a disability or impairment, you might struggle to understand a parent who cannot contemplate caring for that child. You may, however, have experience of coming up against some choice or challenge where you have had to be honest and recognise that there are things that others can tackle but that are just too much for you.

All this, of course, is far too complex to share with young children, but going through the stages at the outset of putting yourself in the birth parents' position and making connections for yourself will make it easier to explain their actions compassionately to your child. When your child is much older you can decide how much of your own personal reactions to your child's history it is helpful to share. Earlier in this book, there was reference to the need to be comfortable with all that is involved with becoming an adoptive parent and especially the reality of the birth family. This does not mean that you are expected to be comfortable with every detail of your child's background. Some information about what may have happened to your child might be uncomfortable. What you need to do is try and make some sense of what happened for yourselves and to get past any initial raw reactions.

Inevitably, the events that have taken place in the lives of many of the older children who are adopted, frequently without their parents' agreement, are very different from the life experiences of their adopters. Confronted with a long history of neglect, abuse and emotionally damaging experiences, adoptive parents have a myriad of questions about how best to support the child and be part of helping her or him to be a survivor. This includes thinking about how to talk about what happened in the past during the years ahead. Part of what you need at the beginning is information not just about **what** happened but also **why**.

- Why was this parent such an angry person and unable to control their anger – perhaps even to the extent where your child has a permanent impairment as a result?
- Why did these parents not learn the difference between healthy sexual relationships and touching children in inappropriate ways?
- Why did these parents get so seriously involved in misusing drugs or alcohol that their life was a disaster, and maybe

their children will continue to struggle with the effects of that misuse?

You are unlikely to get all the answers, but talking about these tough areas with those who know and work with the birth parents will help you find a workable explanation to share with your child. It may be well down the line before your child is ready to look at any of these painful parts of her or his story. Older children who have already some knowledge of past events may go through stages of wanting you to be angry about what has happened to them before being ready to try and understand why it all happened. It will help you to support your child's efforts – perhaps as an adult – to understand their birth parents if you have been down that route yourself at the beginning. If it all feels really difficult, just keep focusing on the fact that you are the adults and your child will need you to be strong for them in the years ahead.

## Keeping written and other information

You may have received information about your child's background in various ways. During the exploration of the link between yourself and your child, you may have seen the main report, such as a Form E or more recently the Child Permanence Report (England) or Child's Adoption Assessment Report (Wales), which was written for discussion of the child's plan at an adoption panel. This is usually a very comprehensive document and will become part of the adoption record your child may see as an adult. Agencies have varied over time in how they provide access to this report and whether they leave it with you. While you will, of course, want to know you have received all the information you might need for the future, this report may not be the best way to hold written information about your child's background. It can graphically lay out the reasons why the adoption plan is necessary, which can be very negative, but leave out some of the day-to-day details and anecdotes that children appreciate. You need to discuss with your social worker the best way for you to receive, keep and use written background material. It is unlikely that this will be shared directly in that form with your child until she or he is an adult, although the content may be explored frequently.

Obviously you will want to keep such information safely and also respect its confidential nature. There can be particularly sensitive areas around information about siblings and extended family members. For some children, part of the evidence supporting their plan for adoption comes from knowledge of what happened to older brothers and sisters. While your child may need to understand at some stage the effect of this on planning for him or her, those other brothers and sisters have their own need for their privacy to be respected. This relates to all information you hold in written form, how you keep it safe and how you share it. Many adoption agencies which provide adoption support, especially those which provide groups for adopted children and young people as well as for adopted adults, report anecdotes of children coming upon material about their adoption by chance. Others at certain times may set out to search the family home for more information if they feel that some is being withheld. You may be right in your assessment that some of the written information you hold is not suitable for a young child but you then need to think about avoiding your child getting the impression you were withholding something from them. You may need to be up front with them that you have formal adult reports, a letter written for them to read when they are about 12 or you have something written by their birth parent for them to read when they are older, that you are happy to share this but think it should wait until the time seems right. You need to be ready to discuss your reasons and also start to share some of what might be there.

Another feature of written reports is often a description of the child and his or her needs. These descriptions of children vary; those about older children may focus on some challenges in their behaviour prior to placement as part of identifying the skills needed in a new family. Some of these reports seem to focus on problems and difficulties or can be light on bringing the child to life as an individual. Try to imagine reading them if they were about you.

Alongside such professional reports about your child, you might have a copy of a feature in a family-finding magazine such as *Be My Parent* or *Adoption Today*. If you first saw your child on a website or on a poster made with the child by a family-finding agency, there are likely to be more personal reasons why you responded to her or his needs. Following on from the questions around 'Why was I adopted?', children wonder about 'Why did you adopt *me*?' Some are curious about why you thought of adopting in the first place and then wonder how you were linked together. They may be reassured that you had a choice – and chose to adopt them. This may lead them to wanting to know about the first information you had about them which prompted you to find out more. What you keep and how you share this can be reassuring. Children can continue to worry about some of the things they believe led to former placements not lasting. If, for example, a child wets the bed sometimes it may help to acknowledge matter-of-factly that you know about that and sort out how it will be handled. Equally it can help children to be open with them about the fact that you know about their background and how life has been for them. This forms a link between what you have in writing and what can be talked about between you.

The other important source of information you are likely to have is a life story book or similar material drawn together to help your child understand his or her background. If your child was young when they joined you, the life story book may have been made by the social worker. Sometimes it does not come with your child if photographs or further information is still being sought. It is important that in the midst of an adoption placement you do not lose track of this. It may be accompanied by or include lots of photographs and stories of your child's time in foster care. It really helps to make sure the names of relatives and friends of the foster carers and friends from nursery or school are all recorded at this stage. These are all the details that parents hold as memories and can so easily be lost for adopted children.

You will need to make decisions about where such material is kept. Children often love looking at photographs of themselves at different ages. It also gives an important message of acceptance and inclusion if photographs of your child before joining your family find a place in the family album. At the same time you need to think about what needs to be kept private. Photographs of birth family members need sensitive consideration, both respecting their confidentiality and also the need for many children to keep such material personally. It is often useful to make copies to keep safe in case such valuable items are lost. While it is right that your child gets the message that life story material and photographs of their birth family are very personal and not to be shared indiscriminately, you need to be sure that this does not mean that important information ends up in the attic or at the back of your wardrobe! Some children might like the idea of a treasure chest for the most important and personal items. If the material suggests that this is best safely locked up, you may agree to look after the key for a small child and can consider as time goes on when your child is ready to take responsibility themselves.

Making life story books with older children often involves many related activities as children explore what it all means for them. Your child should be accustomed to this being treated confidentially during their preparation to move to your family. Careful discussion needs to take place about how and when this material may be shared with you and how this is discussed with your child. A good handover can lay the foundation for how you will continue to use and build on the work already started.

Your child's preparation may also have included use of some children's books. It may be helpful to refer back to these, or they may be part of a series with other relevant stages. For example, if your child is familiar with *Nutmeg Gets Adopted* (published by BAAF), it may be useful to move on to the further stories of Nutmeg. Older children may have been given a copy of *Adoption: What it is and what it means*, a guide for children and young people (published by BAAF) or other written information (see Useful Books). They may find it helpful to talk this over with you.

## Who needs the information?

Exploring all the information that could come with your child and thinking about how you will use it focuses attention on openness and sharing. This needs to be allied not only with how you will keep this information safe, but also with consideration with your child about who in his or her new network needs to know this information, what is appropriately shared when, how and by whom. You need to think about:

- close relatives, eager grandparents;
- other children already in your family;
- close friends who might be your main source of support or may help with care of the child through babysitting;
- interested but more distant friends and relatives;
- nursery, playgroup, school;
- your child's friends;
- neighbours and local community.

Some young children who are secure and well settled with you may be quite happy to share information with others, reflecting the comfortable way you have talked with them. They will need clear guidance on subjects that are best discussed privately, perhaps indicating who to talk to about certain things. Some of this can be modelled on how you respond to questions from other people. You might find it helpful to have a few ready-prepared phrases to respond to other people, depending on whether they are expressing well-intentioned interest or just being nosy!

Children need to learn over time the difference between discretion, including respect for other peoples' privacy, and secrecy which can be risky or unhealthy. Part of growing up is about learning the subtleties around openness; honesty; confidentiality; privacy; good and bad secrets. This needs specific attention for adopted children. What you share needs to go alongside your view of how much of this they have sorted out. Most young children, for example, need to know enough to answer any obvious questions from friends but, unless it is essential, do not need lots of information with "health warnings" about not telling other people. Other children may come with knowledge of life that is well beyond the experience of their peers. They need explicit guidance on safe people to whom they can talk. If there have been concerns about your child approaching others indiscriminately before they came to you, it is particularly important to address this early. As your child grows older, she or he may want to think about whom they could confide in and what may be shared amongst adults.

## Cover stories

When your child makes new friends or meets new people, like teachers or friends' parents, they may ask awkward questions. It is vital that your child has answers ready and does not start making things up which can be so difficult to put right later. Make sure that your child has an explanation ready for the things that may seem odd to an outsider. Being adopted is not something to be ashamed of, but it is something that needs explaining; unfortunately, the general public's view of adoption is often still very old-fashioned. One mother told us, 'My daughter came home from school upset. A child had told her that adoption means that her mum had given her away and had never loved her. She was very hurt and bewildered. She was anxious to hear again how she was adopted, that her mum had loved her so much and had wanted only the best for her but was worried that she could not provide this.' Help your child to be prepared for these kinds of responses and to be ready with answers – answers which are the truth without going into details which are private.

Some children find it easier to talk to their brothers and sisters in their adoptive family. You may need to support these other children in being a communication channel. The children may all have joined you through adoption, so recognition of this can be comforting and supportive. The shared experience of adoption can be enjoyed while leaving each individual child free to make choices about how much of their personal background to share. If you have a "mixed" family of children who joined you in different ways, you may need to discuss this openly while confirming their joint "belonging". Within these situations, children will need a growing understanding of how their uniqueness and differing needs will be recognised. If, for example, a child is upset about something relating to their background or adoption, it can help to suggest saying to a brother or sister that they were distracted, rude or angry because something was bothering them and that they have talked to Mum or Dad about it.

## Thoughts and feelings

*Save every scrap of information you can get your hands on – that's my advice, or at least know where you can lay your hands on it. It isn't just the earth-shattering truths that children want. They have a right to know all those little things like – when did my first tooth come through? And it's so tragic if you can't tell them.*

*It's been a gentle revealing of facts over the years, sometimes softening the truth but never avoiding it if it was necessary to answer the question. Our children trust us to tell them the truth as far as we are able or to try to find out the answer for them.*

*After all we'd heard about his background we weren't that comfortable, to be honest, with meeting his birth parents. I'm glad we did though – it made us a little bit more compassionate and understanding towards them and I'm sure that comes over when we talk to him about his early life.*

*I also remember trying to talk to people about my origins and would ask questions like, 'Why am I black?', or 'Where did my real father come from?'. The answers I would receive would be along the lines of, 'It's nothing to worry about, you are British' or 'England is your home, you are one of us'. These answers may well have been well-meaning, but when I was older I was bitter about them.*

---

*My strong advice to white families offering homes to black children is to be honest with them when they want to talk about such sensitive issues. Don't be afraid to discuss with them their origins or the harsh realities of the world outside. It may well be that such discussions will cause stress or hurt to your child at times, but warmth, love and honesty and really sharing sensitive issues will overcome stress or hurt... Your child will grow and develop and will very likely be a more well adjusted person who is able to face the realities of what life can be like.*

---

# 03

# What children need at different times

*We introduced things gradually to our daughter – the fact that her mother couldn't manage to look after her family of seven children satisfied her at first, but she soon wanted to know why she couldn't manage. This led to the fact that her father was away from home a lot so she had to cope alone. This again satisfied her for a while and*

*she described her father as a "wanderer"…but*
*gradually she wanted to know why he was away*
*so much and we had to tell her that he sometimes*
*stole things and got sent to prison. We tried not to*
*imply that he was a bad man but that he took*
*drugs and needed money to buy them. She is now*
*strongly anti-drugs but seems to feel that people*
*who take them are "silly" rather than "bad".*

In the past, talking to children about their adoption and their family history raised questions about the impact of such information on their emotional development. We now have a lot more knowledge stemming from the work of a psychologist in the USA, David Brodzinsky, who is also himself an adoptive parent. He has explained what children understand in terms of both their cognitive and emotional development. This makes it clear that explaining adoption is something that continues throughout childhood and into adulthood, and what information is needed is linked to recognised stages in children's development. Developing such a framework has made increasing sense to adoptive parents involved in the "telling". People did worry for a while that we might have swung from saying too little too late to overloading children with more knowledge than they could cope with. Some adoptive parents worried too that children who seemed quite happy about their adoption when they were younger began bringing up questions and concerns in later years. We now see this as a very natural stage in the development of understanding.

Just as children may at different times have a range of feelings about their adoption, adoptive parents too are likely to find a variety of emotions triggered at different stages. When you applied to adopt you probably talked about the reminders of fertility issues that can recur. Sometimes this can happen unexpectedly and catch you unawares, but it is in thinking of all the stages of talking about adoption – about your child's birth parents and why you chose to adopt – that you can predict this will come to the fore. From the young child perhaps wanting to "grow in your tummy" through the stages of curiosity and sometimes confusion about these "other" parents, the adolescent anxieties about sexuality and on to thoughts about becoming grandparents, you are likely to be doing your best to say and do what is right for your child. At the same time, you are likely to recognise feelings in yourself that you do not necessarily want to transfer. Where it is a couple who have adopted, this is when it is important to be able to share such feelings and support each other. Close friends and family are often also helpful supports. Single adopters too need to be sure that they have their supports in place for these times, whether they are personal friends or relatives or professional supports.

## Stages in development

So, what are these stages and what do they mean for adopted children and their parents? Children develop at different speeds, so what follows is only a rough guide to the ages at which new developments occur.

### Young children

First of all, small children under four years of age seldom have an intellectual understanding of adoption. However, this does not mean there is no point in introducing the idea. Children's perception develops ahead of their understanding of concepts and at this early stage they are absorbing all sorts of ideas of themselves as separate and different from others. This is a simple but growing awareness of who they are: whether they are a boy or a girl, the colour of their eyes, hair, skin, personal attributes, family roles, what mummies or daddies do, and so on. These differences may have values attached to them as a result of parental connotations and the feelings that come with them. The term "adopted" can fit in here and become another difference which can have "good" or "bad" values attached. Later in this book we will consider more the needs of children who look obviously different from their adoptive parents, particularly those who do not share their parents' ethnicity. What is important to note here is how early children are aware of difference, the beginning of putting values on differences – and the risks around what may be conveyed by **not** speaking about certain areas. So, at this early age, the feelings conveyed around the words spoken are most important, both in creating a positive atmosphere around your child's adoption and also in helping children realise it is an open subject that can be talked about easily.

Of course, this sounds easy, but is not always so in practice. For some adoptive parents, this may be because they have grown so close to the child that it is hard to talk about their having "other" parents or about the fact that the child was not born to them. For others, knowing logically that at a very early age the child only needs very simple limited information does not stop them being anxious about all the more complicated background information that they are going to have to address in the future.

---

## YOUR CHILD'S OWN STORY

Long before your child is old enough to go to school, you will be faced with questions like 'Where did I come from?' All parents are. You can answer simple, direct questions like this with simple, direct answers like 'You grew in someone else's tummy and then you came to join our family'. You can build on this by reading from relevant picture books but, best of all, tell your child's own story, which will almost certainly become a great favourite. If you don't have a life story book for your child, start to put one together. The story – with photographs – of 'The day Mummy (and Daddy) got me' can be used to convey great excitement and pleasure and can be illustrated with any details possible, such as the clothes you all wore, the way you travelled, what the weather was like and what everybody concerned said.

In this situation, people often seek the "right" book to read to their child, which can certainly help. However, if you are really feeling worried, it is best to first sort out the reasons for this so that adult anxieties do not transmit themselves to the child. Then, once you feel comfortable about what you are doing, the most natural way for you will fall into place. This may be the use of a bedtime storybook, but for some people that seems too planned and they prefer to build in opportunities for natural reference to the adoption by looking at photographs, recalling anecdotes of first seeing their child, and so on. Many adopters find it a benefit to practise first, getting used to saying the words, polishing the story without being challenged, growing comfortable with what they are saying and with acknowledging that this child is not born to them.

Once children reach the age of about four, they often ask lots of questions about babies and where they come from. In fact, there are lots of similarities in how children learn about adoption and about reproduction and sexual relationships. Birth and adoption are often mixed up in their minds. At the same time, children are widening their contacts with other adults and children, particularly through playgroups and starting school, and perhaps talking of their adoption. Given that it is difficult to keep fully aware of what children talk about, adoptive parents often need to bear in mind the support available from grandparents and other family members and close friends in confirming the messages given about the adoption; they also need to be ready to respond if their children receive less helpful comments. It helps to suggest words they can use to explain to their friends what adoption is about (you will have read about what we call "cover stories" in Chapter 2).

There is, of course, a world of difference between preparing to introduce the adoption story to a pre-school child who is well settled with you and working out what you might need to begin talking about to one who has only recently joined you. People who have adopted older children will know that it is during these early years that many of their children's ideas and views of themselves have their foundation. If misunderstandings and misperceptions become established, they take a long time to change as the child often cannot put them into words and connections have already been made in their minds when no one was paying attention to what they were thinking. The security of adoption can be hard to comprehend if an adopted person has picked up somehow that originally they were not wanted, maybe because they were "bad" or caused the problems for their birth parents. Sometimes odd unhelpful comments from other people or their own angry thoughts may be put together by children with the disappearance or death of a parent to create misperceptions which they then do not dare to voice to anyone else.

If a child is hiding away with their hands over their ears or diverting you with silly, hyperactive behaviour if you try and approach a sensitive area, you may need extra help to look at ways to deal with this. No one wants to cause a child unnecessary distress and if their feelings become overwhelming, they will not be able to move forward. If you find yourself in this position, you need to think about finding longer-term approaches to help your child sort out hidden fears arising from their past rather than allowing them to become buried. Simply waiting until the child seems "ready" may in reality mean that some areas are avoided. Buried problems can either contaminate healthy growth or may suddenly burst out and cause greater difficulty. You might like to find out more about techniques such as therapeutic story telling which offer more imaginative and fun ways for children to find better solutions to problem areas without confronting them with material which seems too scary. It is always wise to talk through ideas like these with specialists before taking action. They can advise you on what would be helpful for you to do as a parent and when a therapist would be more appropriate.

### School-aged children

From about the age of six, adopted children are likely to have begun to understand at a simple level the meaning of adoption and the different ways of entering a family. This is the starting point for the child for the exploration through the years ahead about family relationships, the permanence of adoptive relationships, the motives both for the adoption and their birth parents' relinquishment of them. This is not a smooth curve; it is like steps and stairs as new stages of development are reached. Children can appear unsettled while they are struggling with a new step and then stabilise for a while before tackling the next hurdle.

A significant step is often around the age of eight. Young children can sometimes shock their parents by their direct way of stating concrete facts that are much more emotive to the adults. But as children mature, they too begin to be more aware of the complexities. Some of this is about the permanence of the adoptive relationship with questions like, 'What if something happens to my adoptive parents?'; 'What if my birth mother's situation changes – can she come back and look for me?' 'If my birth mother could give me away, could my adoptive parents do that too?' Children also begin to learn more about the needs of other people, especially the people most important to them, and may begin to wonder about their birth parents' feelings.

For children who were placed for adoption at a very young age, it is usually not until they are of mid-primary school age that they can really recognise the loss involved in adoption. It is therefore quite normal and natural that children may go through a period described by Brodzinsky as 'adaptive grieving', and for a while they may be confused or uncertain. This can be troubling for adoptive parents who are not prepared for the possibility. The discussions about adoption that seemed so positive earlier now seem to be bringing problems. The children may become more difficult but not want to talk about it. By this stage, if children were placed as babies or toddlers, there will have been many shared family experiences and adoption will seem to have found its place amongst all the normal day-to-day activities. It is not surprising therefore that adoptive parents may become worried by this change or feel that the security they had built up as parents to their child is somehow under question. Think back, however, to the concepts introduced at the beginning and the search for balance between the positives of adoption and recognising the losses. This does not mean that throughout childhood this "yin and yang" are always kept in balance, rather that sometimes one predominates and then there is a period when the focus alters, everything becomes churned up until balance is restored. Sometimes this coincides with a period when children are dealing with more questions, or even teasing at school and perhaps negative remarks about adoption. We know we cannot protect them from wider comments, but we need to be aware that these can add to a child's uncertainty and they may find it hard to share all this with their adoptive parents. Often it helps at this stage to contact one of the growing number of post-adoption counselling services, either to talk through personal issues or locate an adoptive parents' self-help group. This may also provide opportunities for your child to meet other adopted children.

## AIDING CHILDREN'S UNDERSTANDING

A book which looks much more fully at the different stages in children's understanding of sex, reproduction and families is *Flight of the Stork: What children think (and when) about sex and family building*, by Anne C Bernstein. This is based on talking to 3–12-year-olds about how people get babies and how mothers and fathers get to be mothers and fathers. There are strong parallels between the six stages suggested by Anne Bernstein and David Brodzinsky's levels in talking about adoption. The Brodzinsky levels are included in the chapter on adoption and there are also chapters on talking with children about assisted reproduction and stepfamilies.

Now, more than ever, it is important for you to feel comfortable with the circumstances of your child's background and to feel sympathy and concern for the predicament which faced your child's birth parents to begin to explain this to your child realistically. If children feel that their birth parents were "bad" in any way, they sometimes assume that this means they are bad too, or that it is their own fault their parents could not keep them. You will need to be careful with the explanations you use. If you say that the birth mother was too poor to keep your child, they may worry that you would give them up if you fell on hard times. If you say that there was no father to help, they may ask why their friends with single parents have not been given up for adoption. You may, of course, be a single adopter yourself. You will need to balance your understanding of the birth parents' pressures with the reality that everything in the birth family was not rosy, and that adoption was for the best. Just as you will probably have been advised to be careful about saying that a particular action was bad or naughty rather than calling your child "bad", you may need to use a similar approach for their birth parents.

If you adopted an older child – perhaps one who was already of school-age when she or he joined you – she or he will be drawing on real memories and experiences which need to be fitted into the picture. Images and events from the past may crop up, perhaps randomly at first, but your child may now be at a stage when these can be integrated into her or his story in a more meaningful way. Again, this will not be easy, either for you or for your child. Young children are not equipped to sort out all the confusing and worrying things that happened to them at the time, so it is not surprising that when these pictures and snippets of earlier experiences return, they can be unsettling for a while. Children may also now be able to recognise the more ambivalent feelings around events as they get older and see beyond simple concrete messages. This adjustment to reality is one of the hard stages of growth.

Regardless of their age when they joined you, working this out should help children move on to recognising their adoptive parents' "entitlement" to be their parents which comes from all the care they have given rather than the biological link. Giving careful thought to all this should provide a much more secure base of understanding for the adolescent as he or she explores the reasons for adoption that will ultimately lead to a healthy level of understanding in adulthood.

## Adolescence

Adoptive parents are not alone in expressing some trepidation about a possible turbulent phase during adolescence. They do, however, have the added question, 'How much of this is due to adolescence and how much to adoption?' Adolescents have a number of common issues and concerns, for example, the competing pulls of a desire for independence with a fear of separation and finding an accepting place in the adult world; finding out more about themselves, their identity, the sort of adult they will become; dealing with emerging sexuality; concern about physical appearance; learning about forming more adult relationships and fear of rejection, and more. It certainly is not hard to see that aspects of adoption are woven through all these. If, in the middle of this, your adopted adolescent's curiosity about his or her origins reaches a peak, you may be concerned about whether more information or possibly contact with a member of his or her birth family will help sort out the concerns or add to the confusion. Some adolescents can push very hard about this and be very confrontational. Whatever you say may be seen as obstructive. It can really help to bring in an adoption support worker who may be accepted as more objective and can also consider the effect on the birth parent. Increasingly, the emphasis on the role of adoptive parents in sharing information with their child about their adoption and origins focuses on the pre-adolescent period. Adopted adolescents may look to outsiders either to validate what they already know or because they want to sort out their personal identity in a neutral setting.

Within the family, a strong relationship based on openness and trust will certainly help, though it may not feel like that at the time. In addition, you may yourself need more information or contact with someone who has access to extra information and can help in teasing out the different issues. It should help to go over old ground again about how each one of us is unique: we all have our basic inheritance from the people who gave us life; we all have different life experiences, stemming from where we live and the sort of families we grow up in; and we all have different opportunities to explore and use our talents and abilities. All these things – not just one of them – make us the people we are.

One family's experience of talking to their adopted son at different stages of their lives is presented in the chapter later in this book entitled 'Talking to children at different ages and stages'.

Adolescents often prefer to talk to someone other than a parent about things that matter most to them and if this is the case, try not to feel hurt. In fact, many adopted teenagers actually say that they chose to struggle with their angst elsewhere to avoid hurting their adoptive parents. You may also need some independent opportunities yourself to balance all this up and feel secure in the vital part you have played as a parent. This could help you wholeheartedly support his or her explorations to bring together all these aspects of himself or herself without feeling a need to make impossible choices. Many of the doubts, difficulties and dilemmas which arise with adopted teenagers are part of growing up.

Most adopted adolescents, with the support of their adoptive parents, will find their way through this stage. Occasionally some will need some space to sort things out and will try breaking away from their adoptive family. As this is usually a "testing out", it is important to "keep the door open" and often it leads to a much more mature understanding by the young person of what they have received through adoption. Some adolescents can benefit from meeting other young people in the same situation, and this is something which is becoming more available, either informally through links made by their parents through self-help groups, or organised by adoption support services that already run groups for adopted adults. Some young people, particularly those who were older when placed and may have had very unsettling early experiences, may need additional counselling or therapy. This is now well understood by adoption specialists who are happy to be approached about such concerns at an early stage and would not want families to be held back by anxieties that they might be "blamed" or seen as failing.

You could return to the agency which placed your child or contact your local authority about adoption support services. For new adoption placements in England and Wales, there are now regulations about providing an adoption support plan and who is responsible for this. Well established adopters will find that not only have services been developing, but their right to an adoption support service is now recognised in legislation. Again, in England and Wales you will find that you have a right to an assessment of your need for an adoption support service. In Scotland and Northern Ireland you may not be able to quote the same regulations, but you will find that adoption support services are receiving attention, including at government level, and options are growing. In Scotland and Northern Ireland, there is already a statutory requirement to provide adoption support to all parties to an adoption; the difference is that there are now more specific requirements in the legislation for England and Wales (Adoption and Children Act 2002).

---

Renée Wolfs in the Netherlands has written a book for adopters there which gives very detailed guidance on talking to your adopted child. Most adoption in the Netherlands is intercountry, and the book concentrates on this area. The chapter on responding to questions reflects the Brodzinsky ages and stages. Some of the questions and answers are particularly relevant for intercountry adopters in the UK, but could be adapted for our domestic adoption. The discussion and examples include responding to questions and comments. Below is an extract from an as yet unpublished translation of Wolfs' book, which BAAF hopes to publish in 2008.

### From about the age of 3
Where do children come from?
Why did I grow in a Russian mother's tummy and not yours?
Can I get into your tummy?
Was my brother/sister in your tummy?

### From about the age of 4 or 5
Why couldn't my mother take care of me any more?
Why did you adopt me?

Can my mother fetch me again?
Why did you take me with you?
Aren't you my real mother?
I wish that I still lived in the country where I was born.


## From about the age of 7 or 8

Why was I given up for adoption?
Did my mother/father love me?
Why didn't you give my parents money?
Did you buy me?
I wanted to be adopted by other parents
My real mother is probably a lot nicer
Where is my mother/father now? How are my parents doing?
You actually would have preferred to have had a child of your
own.


## From about the age of 9 or 10

I won't listen to you because you are not my real mother.
Why couldn't my parents care for me? (more specific)
Why was I adopted and my sisters and brothers were not?
How much did you have to pay for me? Why can only rich
people adopt?
Are my parents OK? They aren't unhappy?
Why was I adopted and all the other children in the orphanage
were not? That isn't fair.
My sister is lucky because she knows who her real mother is. It
is not fair that I don't know who my mother is.

These questions themselves indicate first of all the changing
and growing preoccupations of children at different ages.
Some questions recur but the answers need to become more
sophisticated. For example, if a four-year-old asks why their
mother couldn't care for them you might have one or two
basic reasons in mind, such as: 'Because in China parents get
punished if they get more than one or two children', or
'Because your mother was far too young to care for a child'. At
seven or eight you might add more details, such as that the

birth parents did not have enough money, were too young, or alone and unmarried, or they may have died. In answering a similar question from a nine or 10-year-old, Renée Wolfs talks both about the child's capacity to know the truth, however painful, and also the possibility of sharing official documents with them. If the child expresses anger, they may be able to distinguish between anger aimed at the birth parent and that aimed at the situation in which they lived. This can lead on to a whole host of other questions.

## Different methods of communication

At the beginning of this chapter, we indicated that these stages of development were a rough guide, and we know not all children reach each stage at the same age. Many of the children placed for adoption have some delays in development, not all of which will be made up. Other children may have a very uneven pattern of development – they may be streetwise well beyond their years and socially very competent but have gaps in schooling and sometimes act like a toddler! Your school-age child may show surprising maturity in some ways, and be able to understand an amazing amount, but still struggle with literacy skills. Some children may have significant disabilities or known impairments. Many of the same ideas can be adapted for all these children.

You will already have learnt about the best ways to communicate with your child, how long he or she needs to absorb information and how to interpret his or her responses. Some children who have limited communication skills may be very sensitive to picking up feelings and atmospheres. Children with physical or sensory impairments may use different equipment or methods of communication and need some extra time, effort and imagination to share their histories. Audio tapes or videos may be more useful for some children, in place of life story books. In the popular BAAF guide, *Life Story Work* (Ryan and Walker, 2007), there is an example of the care taken for a blind child to bring together tactile objects such as buttons from a favourite person's jacket, or shells collected on a particular outing, to help keep his memories. Computers now offer a range of other possibilities along with use of other forms of communication, such as Makaton or Bliss. Recent research on communicating with disabled children suggests that for many there is little difference from communicating with any child in regard to understanding their needs, even if some of the means need to be adapted. Some of the basic skills are not hard to learn, and attitudes are all-important.

Not all social workers are familiar with this area of work, so if your child does have an impairment, you need to check carefully what has been done so far and then pick this up once you are familiar with your child's abilities. Some children with learning difficulties will need repetition of a simple story for longer. Your child may need everything to be clearly personal and naming him or herself rather than being able to make the connections with a story about a puppet, an animal or another child with a different name. Many children, however, may just need a little longer to go through the various developmental stages.

Many children, regardless of whether they have an impairment, may benefit from physically visiting areas where they have lived. This may have already happened as part of the life story work done with your child, but returning to former haunts can both create a further connection for you with your child's world and may help your child to look at past events with fresh eyes now she or he is older.

Play, of course, is an important part of children's lives. Books such as *Life Story Work* suggest various ways of communicating with children through play. These may give you some ideas but, just as your child or children will want you be their parent, not a therapist, so too your use of play needs to be about enjoying time with your child/ren, not about using techniques with them. At the same time, observing and being with your children as they play may offer opportunities that will help you tackle their adoption story. Many children now being placed for adoption are delayed in their use of language. For young children and those with developmental delays, talking as you play helps them to develop language both to share events and name feelings. Children who find it hard to talk to you directly may find it easier to have a conversation through puppets or toy telephones. Letting them describe their pictures to you can tell you a lot. Sometimes pretend play can spark off thoughts that lead to further discussion either at the time or later – perhaps at bedtime with a favourite toy or security blanket firmly grasped.

## Who is my real mummy?

It might help, if your child asks questions like, 'But who is my real mummy?' to in turn ask simple questions like: who puts you to bed? Who takes you to school? Who reads you stories? Who do you feel is your real mummy? Who do you want when you wake up in the night? Of course, you want them to understand about their birth mother too; if you approach it gently, you'll probably find that your child can cope with the idea of two mothers, both real in different ways. A planned approach to talking about adoption allows space to explore areas like "real" parents in a considered way. You may well also need a few one-liners in mind to use in different contexts such as providing your child with a confident response to someone trying to bully or tease them by saying you are not their real mum or dad. Something along the lines of 'Well, they're my real adoptive mum/dad and that's fine by me' might work. Such responses are realistic – and can be adapted by you if your child tries saying you can't tell her or him off because you're not their real parent! What matters is that you find a form of words which is comfortable, deals with the immediate challenge and stands up to more reflective discussion.

While this book is about talking about adoption to your adopted child, the evidence from the rapidly increasing use of adoption support services is that this quest for further knowledge continues through adulthood for many adopted people. Some research completed by Professor David Howe (1996), at the University of East Anglia, on the patterns of adoption shows the long-term effects. Those who have a particularly stormy adolescence may not be able to tackle understanding what their adoption means for them until they are in their twenties. For example, some angry adolescents, after fighting for their independence, may reach the point of "the calm after the storm" when they can experience a more relaxed relationship. Perhaps it is only then that they can accept they were really loved and wanted. (See *Adopters on Adoption* in Useful Books.)

## Thoughts and feelings

*Jason, a black baby with multiple disabilities, was placed with a white foster carer soon after birth. When he was two years old, he was placed for adoption with a single black parent. He repeatedly touched his own skin and then stroked his new mother's face with real pleasure.*
From *Taking Extra Care*, (Argent and Kerrane, 1997)

*There's no question of sitting down and saying 'We've got something to tell you'. The situation is one which is lived out from day to day. The facts filter through gradually, some in answer to questions put usually when you're in the middle of trying to cross a busy road or writing 'Happy Birthday' on a cake, and some you produce yourself whenever the opportunity arises.*

*Our daughter, adopted as a baby, loves to hear her "own" story over and over again with different details added at each telling. Long before she could talk or possibly understand the meaning of adoption, she knew she was our 'darling adopted daughter', while her elder sister was our 'darling daughter'. She was, therefore, always aware of a difference but one that had no bearing on our love for both of them. Later, when she was able to ask about adoption, it was possible to tell her simply and naturally that her sister grew in my tummy whereas she grew in Pauline's tummy.*

---

*We try to be very open with him and keep his life story book handy and answer his questions, but loving him as we do, it does hurt when he suddenly says out of the blue, 'I wish I could still live with Grandma Sadie'. You feel so cruel explaining that it isn't possible and you know he doesn't want to believe you.*

---

*Seven-year-old Donald, who was mycocephalic and had multiple disabilities, would not be separated from his life story. He tore all other books but not this one. Although he could certainly not comprehend the story, he knew it was his. Because it was valued he was proud of himself. He turned the pages carefully and pointed at the pictures and laughed.*

---

*I wrote down a little story for my daughter which I called "Emma is adopted". It's very easy, with a sentence or two on each page, and photographs of her and us. It tells the story of how she came to us in a very simple way, with lots of repeated bits. She's always loved it. At one time we used to have to read it to her half a dozen times a day. Now she's taken it all in, but she still goes back to it sometimes and we build on it and add pages. I can't think of a better way.*
From *Taking Extra Care*, (Argent and Kerrane, 1997)

---

*Sally, aged 11, had seen her single mother taken away in an ambulance and knew she was dead because people said so. Sally had learning difficulties and no concept of death. She was not taken to the funeral because no one wanted to upset her. As far as she was concerned her mother had not come back because she was cross. Only much later, when she was taken to see the grave, did she understand why her mother could not look after her any longer. She could then begin to relate to her dead mother and to move into the future.*
From *Taking Extra Care*, (Argent and Kerrane, 1997)

# 04

# Some difficulties in talking

*We had to help Joanna cope with the fact that her father had sexually abused her. We started to talk about different kinds of love, about the way mummies and daddies love each other being different from the way children love parents and parents love children. We explained that some grown-ups get things muddled up and don't have the same rules as other people. We said, 'When*

*your daddy was young his daddy loved him in the
way that mummies and daddies love each other, so
he thought it was okay to love you like that. But
that is wrong and I know it's wrong and you knew
it was wrong and that's why you told your teacher.*

---

## Starting or building the history when your child is older

While this book is encouraging you to start talking about adoption
very early with your child to allow for a gentle, natural progress
through the stages, sometimes this does not happen. What should
you do if you are now feeling you should have started sooner?
Sometimes people find the first stage of introducing the basic fact
of adoption at an early age fairly straightforward but then all the
other aspects of childhood take over and suddenly the child is ready
to start secondary school and not much more has been discussed.
This can feel especially worrying if you have some written
information that you were notionally expected to be sharing at this
stage. For other adopters, new unanticipated information may have
emerged after the adoption which was not shared with the child at
the time but is still hanging in the background.

As long as you are not being pushed by some urgent outside
pressures, it is best to think everything through carefully
beforehand. The main thing is to get over the initial hurdles before
they become too big. This involves first of all sharing why you left
introducing the subject or building on the information until your
child was much older. Sometimes people say either that if things
were going well they did not want to disturb this, or if life was a bit
more fraught, that they did not want to make it worse. That might
seem reasonable, but the perfect time may never come! You need
to think about the anxieties that may lie behind this approach. If
you felt that you should wait until he or she was old enough to
understand it fully, you will need to explain that to your child, and
be ready to counter any impression that you did not want to tell the

truth or felt that there were uncomfortable secrets that you really did not want to share. You may need to acknowledge that your child could see this differently and accept that with hindsight you should have started sooner but you did what you thought best at the time. Earlier in this book there was reference to triggers for children. Similarly, for you as adults, there may be some event or incident that was the trigger in deciding that you need to share more information with your child now. This may provide an opportunity to introduce the subject and get started.

Sometimes people are very conscious of how emotional they can become in talking to their child. It is not surprising that if a young child is saying that they wish they had come out of your tummy – and you feel that too – it is hard to follow suggestions like letting her or him act out being your baby, sharing any sadness helpfully and gently helping your child feel comfortable with their reality. Try to choose a time when you are feeling emotionally strong and involve your partner or someone you trust to provide support.

Sometimes with two adoptive parents, they may have different views of the "right time" or how to approach some parts of a child's story. You need to talk this out between you both to enable you to be consistent in what you say and also so you are both ready to answer further questions. If older children feel that people held back the truth, they may also need to check facts with other trusted adults such as grandparents as well. If you are anxious that you might have to talk about your infertility or details about the birth parents that you are unsure about sharing, it is as well to explore in advance the sorts of words you might use that you will feel comfortable with and your child will understand.

What might be the differences in telling your child about their adoption at a later stage? First of all, you cannot just slip words like adoption into more general conversation. It is not like familiarising a young child with a word that has not already got a real meaning for them. An older child is likely to have already associated meanings and values with the word whether this is the first time it has been associated with themselves or if they knew of their adoption but their perception has been influenced by an impression that you found it hard to bring up the subject again.

We know from adopted adults who have come together and reflected on how they heard about their adoption, a number who heard first in the 7–16 age range experienced a strong sense of shock and trauma, some describing every detail of where they were in an unforgettable way. This, of course, is about the impact of suddenly learning such important facts about themselves when old enough to have some idea of what they mean – it does not mean that they have absorbed all the information that may have been given to them. Initially you may be confronted with silence and disbelief, or your child's anger and upset, all of which need to be acknowledged before moving on to more discussion. Although your child may have reached a stage where he or she will have some understanding of the information you are sharing, this does not mean that your child can take it all in immediately; information will need to be built up in stages just as if you had started earlier. Some of the implications may be clear to your child at once but many questions are likely to come later so that once the door is opened, it needs to be kept open wholeheartedly and opportunities explicitly given for further discussions.

Sometimes people feel more confident if, as well as ensuring starting in a relaxed atmosphere in privacy and with no interruptions, some additional steps are prepared, for example, having photographs or other reminders of your first meeting with your child. You might also have suggestions ready about what can be made available to your child when they are ready for the next steps. You may have a letter from the birth parents or the written background information aimed at your child's current age. There may be opportunities to talk to others like grandparents who shared the early days of the adoption placement. Such possibilities, if offered, can help to reassure your child that you can be trusted to share the truth with him or her even if he or she is not ready for all of it immediately. If you think that previously your child might have thought you were reluctant to follow up with further discussions, then you will need to demonstrate a change and have concrete ideas about doing this. If your child does not say much you need to be sure that after giving her or him some space you check within a day or two whether they have had further thoughts. You may need to take the initiative on a number of occasions if they are going to be really reassured that now you are willing to talk with them.

## It's OK to be angry

If you have been discussing something painful and your child is angry, it is important to recognise this directly with them. You may already have helped your child establish non-destructive ways to express angry feelings about the usual childhood frustrations, so give them space for this or be ready with suggestions. Acknowledging possible feelings and indicating you can identify with them through comments like, 'I would be angry/upset too if that had happened to me', or just a caring touch or gesture will help your child feel less alone with her or his feelings. Let them cry if they need to. Cry with them, if you want to and that feels natural. As the adult, however, you need to be aware of when enough is enough – your child will need to know not only that you are picking up her or his feelings but also that you can contain these and will not let them get out of control. You do not need to feel you've dealt with everything in one conversation, and that would probably be too much for your child too. What is most important is that your child is given opportunities to return to the subject and that you check this rather than leaving the initiative with your child. No matter what you say about coming to talk to you at any time, many children still find it difficult to do this. They may pick up any natural discomfort as meaning it is really hard for you to talk about part of their story and not wish to cause you further upset.

## Telling particularly distressing facts

There are some facts that will always be very difficult to face. There will, of course, be differences in addressing distressing backgrounds with children who were placed at a very early age with no direct experience of life with their birth family and those who spent time in a chaotic or dangerous household.

## Difficult backgrounds

For children placed as babies, the hard parts may be about the circumstances surrounding their conception. Some of the reasons why birth mothers cannot face bringing up their children are particularly painful. Think of a young teenage girl who is pregnant as a result of abuse by a family member, or a young woman who has been raped. We now are also beginning to see asylum seekers who have horrendous stories to tell – and are also pregnant as a result. The early stages of explaining your child's adoption need not go into details of this but at a later stage your child may wish for more and begin, for example, to question what is known of their birth father. Awareness of the part played by the birth father becomes much clearer to children as they make sense of reproduction. You need to keep in touch with the work that schools are doing in both sex education and social and personal development. Once children reach puberty, sexual issues become more highly charged. Ultimately your child may find out the full story which led to their adoption through seeing their records or may be plunged into a raw account by tracing their birth mother.

So, how do you help your child understand a difficult truth? First of all you think about how a child might feel if they pick up that their birth mother could not bear to keep them because of how they were conceived. As adults we can understand the mother's revulsion at the act which created the child  and separate that from rejection of the child. Your child may not manage that so well without your help. She or he will need to know that you can accept the information which led to her or his existence and have wholeheartedly accepted her or him as an individual free from that original act. An indication that the birth mother was not a willing participant in the events leading to the pregacy may be sufficent – at least as a starting point. Your sensitivity to your child will guide you about how much more would be helpful. What you will need to be prepared for is the way your child's ability to deal with information is likely to change as their knowledge of the world develops. For a young child, for example, being made or forced to do something will probably be related to their normal day-to-day experiences. Older children will begin to pick up through the media and more formally though education about issues such as keeping safe, risks of abuse and various social problems.

As you help your growing child learn about appropriate sexual boundaries, it will also help if you have made some sense yourself of how realities like rape or incest can happen and the context leading to force or abuse. This is not about condoning wrong behaviour. Sometimes, in counselling adults who were adopted many years ago, we meet individuals who still harbour bitter, angry feelings towards a birth parent, such as judging a woman, who could not name the father of her baby, as a "slut". For the individuals who cannot get past such feelings or temper their moral judgements with compassion, that bitterness can damage their lives. You will be more able to support your child if you have sorted out your own feelings.

As already suggested, if your child was rejected as a baby or was abused before being taken away from his or her parents, you will need to try to put yourself in those parents' place. Their circumstances may have been impossible for them to cope with. Try to imagine how you would feel if you had never had a loving relationship with anyone or if you were faced with a combination of poverty, loneliness, unemployment, inadequate housing and so on: you too might be driven to breaking point. Of course, it is one thing to accept distressing facts as a mature adult, but much more difficult to convey them to a child in an acceptable way. But however inadequate you feel your child's parents may have been, there are always good points: try to find these out and emphasise them to your child. Talk about the parents in simple language the child can understand and, if you can accept the facts, it will be that much easier for the child to accept them too and forgive the parents. One adopter told us, 'Children can accept anything if you tell them in the right way; it's the grown-ups who find things difficult to accept'. It is also worth bearing in mind that, in certain cases, young people will feel better if they know that their adoptive parents do not condone the behaviour of a birth parent; for example, domestic violence leading to the killing of the mother by the father is bad and must be recognised as such. What is important is that your adopted child knows that you love, trust and believe in them regardless of what has happened in their birth family. If your child is still quite young, a recent book from BAAF – *Spark Learns to Fly* – might help as it includes domestic violence, recognises the feelings and dilemmas for children and ends with a positive note as Spark learns a new skill (see Useful Books).

Putting difficult facts into words, however, is not easy. Your language will need to change as time goes on to recognise your child's development. You will be the best judge of your child's understanding, but it helps to have ideas of the next steps in an explanation so that you feel prepared. You may, for example, find it enough with a small child to talk of a birth parent being "unwell" and then be ready to move on to an explanation of "good medicine" and "bad medicine" if a parent misuses drugs. You can then help your child understand that this "bad medicine" could have muddled their brain and led them to do things that were silly or wrong, or not be able to care for a baby. Your child may have come to you later with their own words for what they have seen or heard about. A little listening or a few gentle questions may help you get started with a young child who knows what happened when their birth parent drank "bad juice". During primary school years, children begin to become familiar with what is meant by "drugs" and "alcohol", especially if schools are addressing these issues. It is useful to keep in touch with what is happening at school as teachers may not be aware of what could be stirred up for your child. Becoming more aware through education of the dangers of certain lifestyles may make your child feel unsettled but she or he may find it awkward or embarrassing to bring this up directly. If you pick up that your child is bothered by something you may need to do a bit of "detective work" and then discuss this with your child. This again is where you need to take the initiative rather than waiting for your child to ask.

Concern about drug misuse is both more routinely addressed at school and a significant factor in the background of children placed for adoption now. You may have to deal with this in a number of different ways. For example, comments from others at school or television programmes may raise worries for your child that they might end up like their birth parent. You need to have both a ready response to deal with an immediate question or comment and access to more detailed information. If you can say confidently that you know your child's birth mother or father took drugs but you are now her or his parents, which gives her or him a different experience and example, then you are demonstrating your belief that she or he has a choice in the route they follow. Preparation for such eventualities not only helps with immediate challenges but also makes a clear statement to your child that you believe in them. This needs to be followed up with real information about lifestyles – possibly at an earlier age than with other children. You will also need guidance for yourselves and your child about addictions.

When, as prospective adopters, you first heard about your child, if he or she was born to drug misusing parents you may have heard about any initial health problems resulting from withdrawal or prematurity. You may also have received information about possible longer-term effects. It is likely to be many years later when you need to update your knowledge to address all the other questions that come up as you talk to your child about his or her background. We are constantly learning more about the effects of parental drug misuse on children as they grow up. While much of this is about the influence of the environment, there may be other aspects causing these children to be more vulnerable than their peers. There are now numerous projects supporting children and families where drug misuse is a problem. While this may no longer be directly relevant to your child, you may pick up some useful ideas for supporting your child in making better choices for themselves. Using general educative information and other such resources in a non-threatening and planned way will provide a base for later times when your child may be going through a difficult patch, especially during adolescence. Such issues may then come up again in a more sudden or dramatic way. It also gives you space to reflect on the differences between the birth parents' circumstances which may have led them to substance misuse and your child's own experiences and supports. This should fit well with other efforts you may be making to encourage your child to look at choices they have in life and help them gain a sense of personal control as they grow towards adulthood.

It is worth remembering that, in the midst of all the concerns about drugs, alcohol misuse has been a long-standing issue in the background of children placed for adoption. While there are some similarities with drug misuse, there is more awareness now of the risks of alcohol misue leading to Foetal Alcohol Effects. As well as understanding the pressures on birth parents – in particular, mothers – you may also need to be very sensitive to the reality that your child may become aware that she or he needs extra medical and educational monitoring or support as a result of that mother's lifestyle. It is worth thinking here about how your child perceives your understanding and compassion towards others who do not cope well with their lives, so this is not just about their individual story. You will also need to help them understand about unintentional consequences of actions and that their birth mother would not have knowingly caused them damage.

Domestic violence and abuse – both physical and sexual – sadly occur in the backgrounds of a number of children placed for adoption. You should be receiving support, advice and, if necessary, access to therapeutic services to help your child survive the effects of this on their development. Most parents understand stages of development like the "terrible twos". Part of the parenting task is to guide children towards acceptable social behaviour including what they can or cannot do when they are angry and the difference between good and bad touching. Helping children learn about limits on behaviour in a caring way and what can get them into trouble with others will also equip them to understand when you try to explain that their birth parents did not learn enough about those limits. The birth parents' history may give you clues as to why they struggled to understand or act within the social boundaries that most people recognise. Older children may need to explore more of this to try to work out some answers to all those questions beginning with "why". You may find that you will need to talk a lot more about acceptable behaviour and the consequences of overstepping the limits than parents whose children have always been in a healthy environment. Getting into the habit of making clear and positive comments on desirable behaviour and not assuming your child has absorbed the rules as you go along is all part of developing your way of communicating all sorts of aspects of the reasons for adoption.

Occasionally, children are placed whose backgrounds include events that attracted media interest. It is particularly important that you have got "behind the headlines", and understood what may have led to a family tragedy. Once you have absorbed all the information, you can begin to think about how much detail needs to accompany the truth. Some young children can accept difficult facts if put in a reassuring manner but may dwell on them once older. A slow gentle growth of understanding is indicated with space for children to say, 'I know enough, I don't need any more'. Some adopted children or adults might ask about newspaper cuttings. It is probably best only to keep those that give a balanced report or might aid understanding. While children are entitled to know the truth of their background, they also have the right to decide how much detail they need. It is important not to rush this and take time to observe the impact of telling different stages of their history.

Some of the children now being placed for adoption have genetic conditions. If a child already has an inherited disability, they will be growing up with the implications of this and their knowledge of their condition will evolve. Often there are support groups linked with different medical conditions which can help with this. As you have chosen to adopt your child, your attitude to disability will emerge. As they grow older, they are likely to learn also about the range of other attitudes to disability and somewhere within that they may need help to understand the particular circumstances of their birth parents. While their birth parents may also have been vulnerable and have struggled to care for other children as well, it is particularly hard for some children to learn they have brothers and sisters doing well at home. It may be that over time some level of contact can ameliorate hurt feelings and help both the birth parents and the child reach a healthier understanding of each other.

The dilemma with other children is that they may be healthy while they are children – the risks are for the future. It continues to be difficult to find families for children with a background of schizophrenia – which is also usually at least part of the reason for the adoption plan. It is one thing to explain why parents with a mental illness could not cope and another to address the personal risk to their child. Some other serious conditions such as Huntingdon's Chorea have similar difficulties. At some point you may need to call upon a geneticist to check the most up-to-date information in a rapidly changing field. Genetic counselling and even testing may be a possibility but only when a child is old enough to make his or her own decisions. Much of this is too complex for a young child to understand but what you can do is to think consciously about your own attitude to life that enabled you to adopt your child. How you deal with risk, handle problems if they crop up and get the most out of each day of your life will all provide a solid value base to share and support your family through whatever lies ahead. You may also have relevant personal life experiences that add to this.

### Helping children who spent time in stressful households

Older children may, of course, have their own memories of family dramas. They may have directly observed traumatic or upsetting events or been on the receiving end. You should know at the beginning of the adoption placement how much your child has shared already. This will give you valuable information about how your child might indicate the need to talk; what works, or doesn't, in response; and whether there are "triggers" to be aware of. For some children, for example, certain times of the year, such as Christmas, have bad associations. You may want to be explicit with your child about knowing what has happened to them or why certain times or events are hard for them and how they might indicate the need for talk – or extra reassurance – but then leave them space.

You may, however, be parenting a child about whose earlier experiences there have been many concerns and suspicions but no direct evidence. "Telling" distressing facts may be one issue but you may at a later date be a vital "listener". It can be a real shock when a child is finally secure enough to begin to share difficult memories for the first time. We might like to think we could find the right words for these situations but logically we know there is no easy answer. What you can do is:

- keep listening;
- acknowledge your child's courage in beginning to talk;
- accept whatever feelings are expressed about it;
- try not to be overwhelmed, or at least don't show it. You will be the best judge of whether your child can accept a hug at such times or needs you to share his or her distress. Remember she or he could only share because it felt safe enough – that sense of safety needs to continue;
- think about whether there is someone you will need to share this with – whether a partner or a professional – and see if you can open up such "next steps".

It may also be helpful to go back to the agency which placed your child with you. There may be a lot more questions that come to mind now. Services that were called in because of an adult drama may not have considered that a very young child in the household could have been aware of what was happening. Knowing more details may explain some of a child's reactions to some trigger noises or actions. Sometimes children in these circumstances make their own connections which are not accurate or contain elements of fantasy – knowing more detailed information can help guide your responses. It is also worth knowing whether, in a family upset, there was someone familiar and trusted available to reassure your child. Just think how bleak it would be to be scared and confused and with no one to hold you or comfort you. If you discover your child was in that position then, you will need to be more active now in showing them that you will be there for them whenever you would expect them to need you. Their experience will not lead them to expect or look for that. This is where talking – or listening to – a child who has been in a distressing situation is different from sharing difficult background information with a child who was removed from a risky environment.

If you feel that the problem is just too big for you to handle, you might find it helpful to talk it over with another parent who has been in a similar position. Other adoptive parents may be contacted through the numerous self-help groups now established in many parts of the UK. The adoptive parents' support organisation, Adoption UK (see Useful Organisations), has local organisers in most parts of the UK and also has a Resource Bank called PAL which helps families contact others who have faced similar dilemmas to theirs. You should also consider whether your child is at a stage where some extra therapeutic help is required. This is not just about specialist skills – it can be safer for children to start dealing with some of the messier parts of their lives outside the family without threatening their hard-won security. They need you to be there for them as a **parent**. If you feel that a trained counsellor could help you, the agency which placed your child or one of the post-adoption counselling services that are now much more widely available may be able to help (see Useful Organisations). If you adopted some time ago, you will find there is growing emphasis throughout the UK on post-adoption support. Recent regulations introduced in England and Wales provide a statutory basis for you to ask for an assessment of your post-adoption need for support services and a plan to be drawn up based on that.

## Lack of information

For some people, the most distressing fact is that they have no information to give their child. This may be because your child was abandoned as a baby. We can only imagine the distress of the mother in such circumstances but all you might have to share with the child may be a few newspaper cuttings or perhaps a piece of clothing or something left with the child. The responsibility that all adoptive parents take on of giving their child security and a sense of belonging with their whole extended family and also developing their child's personal self-confidence will be particularly important for these children who will always have a missing piece of their personal jigsaw. The charity Supporting Adults Affected by Adoption: NORCAP has a subgroup for foundlings – see Useful Organisations.

Although circumstances may be different and there may be general knowledge of social pressures, intercountry adopters can face similar gaps in information of the child's personal history. The best you may be able to do is recognise this with your child and share with them all the efforts you made to find out as much as possible at the time. Make sure you have left information about how you can be contacted if further information emerges. You might try using 'I wonder...' type questions, such as 'I wonder if your mother/father was tall or had green eyes like you?' or 'I wonder if your mother thinks of you when your birthday comes around?' Comments like this show you are thinking about your child's concerns and make a clear statement that your child did not appear from nowhere but has a history and background, even if at this stage you do not know it. If it helps your child they could draw a picture of what they think their birth parents might have looked like to put in a family album. Some gesture like lighting a candle before their birthday to indicate they were thinking about their mother and hoping she is at a happier point in her life could also help some children. As the parent, when you bring this up you need to be alert to what might comfort your child, even if this is tinged with sadness.

### If your child's adoption was contested

Your child's birth parent(s) may have wanted to keep the child, but for many different reasons may not have been allowed to do so. Perhaps the birth parents were considered unable to bring up a child adequately or safely, and the court agreed that the risks were too great for the child to return to them. Whatever the reason for this, you have a delicate task ahead. While your child may not feel rejected, he or she may go through a phase of feeling that his or her birth parents were treated unfairly by you as well as by the state. They may even wonder if they were stolen! Your best bet is to keep showing your love for your child and your sympathy for the birth parents' predicament, while accepting the fact that what was done was for the best. Over time your child will need to learn more about how such decisions are made.

If your child has a life story book, this is a useful starting point. This will have been written at a particular point in time and will probably be a very general summary of what the child may have experienced. It may also include photographs or details of social workers and others who were key to the decisions made before your child joined your family. Older children may have graphic pictures in their minds linked to that summary. It is useful in going through this information, not just to read it but to check your child's understanding of what is written. Sometimes adoptive parents can be quite taken aback by young children's very blunt way of talking about problems like a parent's abuse of alcohol, but if your child is going to be able to deal with this, you must also be able to. This can help you find out ways in which the life story book needs to be added to in the future, both with the child's new experiences within your family and his or her growing understanding of their past.

Depending on where in the UK you live and when you adopted, you may have been involved in a contested court case, or the court may have ruled against the birth parents' opposition before your child came to live with you. Legislation has been changing in the different legal jurisdictions in the UK and both this and social work practice will continue to change and develop as society struggles to balance the rights of birth parents with the best interests of children. Regardless of whether you go through an actively opposed court case when your child is already living with you or the legal situation is fairly straightforward, the actual legal steps can raise more questions. You may need to explain the details of the court process and the visit of the Children's Guardian, or in Scotland the curator ad litem. If your child is old enough to be aware of this, it can be a very unsettling time for him or her as well as causing you anxiety. Of course, your social worker and legal representative will be actively involved in supporting and guiding you.

Your child will also need to be able to discuss what is happening with you. In these situations it is usually best to make it clear that while their views and wishes are important and the court will want to hear about them, the decisions will be taken by the adults. Some children at such a time can feel very conflicting loyalties and need a lot of reassurance that they are not being asked to forget or reject their birth parents. Some can feel that they are being asked to make choices or that in order to convince everyone where they want to be, the adopters need to be all "good" and their birth parents "bad". This does not help in the longer term with a healthy integration of their two families as part of their identity. Sometimes talking to someone outside your family, not personally involved, can be easier for your child.

Legal procedures are often complex so it may be useful to have a simple written outline to retain of how the decisions for adoption were made and how differing opinions were taken into consideration. Your child may want to find out more about this in the future. This is likely to be particularly useful if you adopted a child from a different part of the UK where some procedures are unfamiliar to you. It may also help to include in any letter from the social worker provided for later use some additional information about this stage. Some birth parents may embark on opposition to the plan but then not follow through or appear at court. This is often because deep down they know the plan is the best for their child but they cannot bring themselves to "sign them away". This is the sort of information that may be helpful in the future in explaining what happened but may not be so clear in official adoption records.

## LEGAL DIFFERENCES

Apart from the fact that historically law in Scotland has different origins from the rest of the UK, well before devolution legislation covering various subjects for both Scotland and Northern Ireland was passed separately from that for England and Wales. Clearly, legal changes go along with developing practice and attitudes towards adoption. This can mean that the law in different parts of the UK may be similar but introduced at different times or that varying responses are found to developments that need legal change. As an example, the concept of "freeing" a child for adoption was introduced as part of the Adoption Act 1976 for England and Wales, in the Adoption Act 1978 for Scotland and in the Adoption (Northern Ireland) Order 1987. Over time, difficulties and delays emerged in the use of freeing. As part of a major overhaul of legislation for England and Wales, freeing came to an end and a new order – a Placement Order – was introduced in the Adoption and Children Act 2002. In Scotland, a review of legislation led to a different solution in the Adoption and Children (Scotland) Act 2007 with the introduction of a Permanency Order which could be used in planning adoption but also in other forms of permanence.

At that point, initial discussions were still ongoing in Northern Ireland about what changes may be introduced, so freeing will continue there for a longer time. Although legislation for England and Wales is the same, the regulations and guidance that follow on from that legislation are produced separately so there may be variations in details of the implementation.

One of the biggest longstanding and continuing differences involves the Children's Hearing system in Scotland, which has a very different approach to compulsory intervention in children's lives from that used in other parts of the UK. For older children, what matters is that wherever they come from in the UK – or indeed from other countries – they should understand that the decision for their adoption was made carefully and was legally robust.

If you are interested in knowing more about the current legal positions in the different parts of the UK, the websites for the Welsh Assembly, the Northern Ireland Assembly and the Scottish Government give useful information. In England, adoption information is available on the website of the Department for Education and Skills. To find the most up-to-date sites, it is usually easier to start with a specialist adoption site, such as the BAAF website, and use the links given there as names can change. Intercountry adopters are likely to have information about the particular country from which they hope to adopt. This should include not just requirements about prospective adopters but also information about how that country ensures that adoption is the best plan for a child.

### Thoughts and feelings

*You need to start as early as possible...by the time John (who had been battered as a baby) was two-and-a-half he knew who had hit him and where the bruises were and who'd seen them and that was why he was taken away. We said, 'Well, when you were only three weeks old you used to cry a lot and your first mummy and daddy thought you were being naughty and they smacked you hard, hard enough to make very big bruises and then the nurse came and saw them and thought they shouldn't smack such a little baby so you were taken away and given to parents who wouldn't smack you. Your first mummy and daddy were very young and they didn't know that little babies aren't being naughty when they cry but cry because they're hungry and want to be cuddled.*

# 05

# Memories

*Baby adopters often have very limited information and it's OK to go back to the agency and ask for more. Our son came to us when he was eight weeks old. We made a book about those first eight weeks (very slim!) but we had to ask the adoption agency for more to put into it. A social worker went off to the hospital where he was born, which was 200 miles away from us, and took a photo for us! We went back to the agency and were able to read more information in the file. It helped fatten the book a little more! Our photocopy of the birth certificate is the most treasured bit of it now that he's 16.*

Children who remain with their birth families throughout childhood have many ways of knowing about their past and their origins. Their parents and relatives, including older brothers or sisters, have memories and stories to tell. During childhood some of these stories become part of the family history, to be brought up and laughed about or wondered over again and again. Often there are photograph albums or sometimes homemade videos of the child at different stages of growing up. Most people know if they were born in hospital, or at home, and many know the time of birth and who was involved, for example, if a friend or relative helped look after any other children in the family at the time. As children grow up, other events like moving house, going to nursery school, holidays, accidents, illnesses, friendships and family celebrations like birthdays and weddings all become part of the family folklore of shared experiences.

For children separated from their birth parents, especially when they are older than babies, it is different. They have no family "keepers of their personal history" who have known them from birth. They have to rely on outsiders like social workers, foster carers or staff at children's homes and hospitals, and medical records. For these children – perhaps like your adopted child – their past is often a mystery or a jumbled collection of memories that no one can ever precisely put into place. One of the important tasks of adoptive parents is to help children integrate knowledge and stories of their birth family with their growing store of memories of events in their adoptive family. Your own perception and recollection of your childhood is likely to be built on a mix of conscious memories and what you have been told. Part of this will happen naturally for your child as they become part of your family; the rest you need to think about consciously. This might be about sometimes using opportunities to refer to birth relatives or stories from before your child joined your family, as well as references to your own extended family and activities you all did together. You might like to have a special folder or container to keep special photographs, mementos and anecdotes from as much of your child's life as possible. Tangible reminders are a good way to recognise and value memories – young children and children with some impairments might particularly enjoy familiar sounds on tape or the feel of objects collected on a special day out.

As well as information about your child's early history, you may also pick up a flavour of what is valued within your child's wider birth family. As your child builds his or her personal identity, this can play a part too. Apart from anecdotes about individual ancestors, there may be special family traditions or over generations many birth family members might have followed a certain trade or craft. For children with parents from different minority ethnic groups, there is likely to be history of movement between countries, such as from Africa to the Caribbean and to Britain, possibly over generations. This type of knowledge is accessible to children within their birth families but if you do not share your child's heritage, some more information from birth relatives can help answer questions that may be prompted by comments outside your family.

## Life story work

Luckily, social workers and others involved now realise that helping children understand and come to terms with what went on in their early lives is the best way to enable them to come to terms with the present and move forward into the future. As referred to earlier, your child should arrive with a life story book or similar material. This may not necessarily include all the day-to-day events, outings or special times shared with their birth parents. If you have the chance to meet the birth parents or other relatives, they might be able to fill in more about their personal recollections or they could be approached when any raw feelings have settled. They may appreciate you understanding and valuing such memories. Some life story books contain limited material and can therefore offer great potential for you and your child to work on together over the years. Even if there is plenty there, sharing memories is an important part of your relationship. Many children, for example, enjoy going through old family albums, or family photographs on the computer. Many of these will reinforce your child's place in your family but including early ones from before your child joined you makes the connection for them and helps them understand their lives as a whole.

If you decide to make a life story book with your child, you could invest in another BAAF book which discusses the subject in much greater detail and offers lots of practical advice and guidance. *Life Story Work* (new edition 2007), by Tony Ryan and Rodger Walker, includes various suggestions for clarifying your child's past – making maps of the local area with moves marked, playing with dolls and models to indicate family members, drawing up family trees, and much more (see Useful Books). BAAF also publishes *My Life and Me*, a life story book designed to be completed by children with help and support from appropriate adults. Colour-coded sections include space for drawings, photographs, documents and a record of thoughts and feelings at various stages in the child's life (see Useful Books). An interactive CD titled *My Life Story* is also available (see Useful Books). There are also plenty of commercially available activity books for children to record family life but you should look through these carefully first as they may bring up complications for an adopted child. It is usually better to make your own book which can be tailored to your child's individual story.

If your child joined you past babyhood, you will also need to depend on your child's memory and on the contacts you have who can help you, in particular workers at the adoption agency who placed your child with you and all her or his previous temporary carers. If you use a loose-leaf folder, you can add to it as more details emerge. It also enables the child to remove any particularly private bits before showing any book or album to friends or relatives.

Some adoption agencies arrange "life appreciation days" in preparation for a child moving into an adoptive family. This is a way of gathering together a whole range of people who have known your child over the years and sharing all their different pieces of information. You will usually go away, not only with your head full of information and stories, but also with pictures and a time line of your child's life.

## Bad memories

Remember that this may not be an easy task. Your child may not want to remember some of his or her early experiences, but to fully explore a child's history or make a life story book all known facts should eventually be covered. You would be well advised to talk to the social worker who worked with your child before you start. Your child may get angry during the time you are exploring their history and may take it out on you, the old hurt and bewilderment coming back. But you are undoubtedly the best person to do this, as you know your child better than anyone else does now, and you have the opportunities that no one else has. You can choose the times when your child is in the right mood. You can continue for as short or as long a time as you want. And, because you are now your child's family, you can do this task from a safe, secure base. You can use these times with your child for building on the warm loving relationship of the present. And as you come up to date, you will be adding the memories of the present to those of the past. It often helps to be able to move around between past and present as a straight chronological approach may be too difficult for your child.

While much of this chapter is about building memories to help your child's knowledge and understanding of his or her history and identity, some memories might be so painful or confused that they can interfere with your child's progress. It is too glib to suggest you could or should help your child to forget difficulties from the past; however, sometimes these intrude before your child is ready to handle them. If your child cannot put these difficult thoughts into words, you may be able to acknowledge that you know they are there and it is too soon to talk, but together you can explore ways to make your child feel more calm and relaxed at such times.

If your child can begin to talk to you about their difficult memories, you may be able to record them in some way and then put them away safely, perhaps locked in a drawer in your room. You can then assure the child that you can contain such memories safely, you both know they are there and can look at them again at a later date if and when your child is ready. You may also want to consult a specialist or therapist about when would be a helpful time for the child to explore aspects of her or his past. Often, children in this position find it really important to keep their home as a "safe place", and feel more comfortable addressing their worrying memories elsewhere.

Sometimes your child's memories can trigger thoughts of events in your own past. Ultimately, a time may come when it will help your child to know just how well you understand what has happened to her or him. Sometimes, if it is too early in your relationship or you are feeling very emotional yourself, this may be too much. The most important part for your child is that she or he feels safe and not overwhelmed by bad memories – to either their own or yours. Approaching these areas slowly gives children confidence that they can manage each step, just as you can. It is a bit like cutting the monsters in the cupboard or under the bed down to size. You do it step by step, and hand in hand until you are ready to face them completely.

If you are developing a life story book and some parts might be upsetting to your child, it is a wise precaution to make copies of photographs and important documents, especially letters. It is not unknown for life story books to be "lost" or destroyed. Of course, books are not the only means of keeping memories and some children may specially value having a safe place in which to keep other items. These may be from the past – perhaps a toy or piece of clothing or gifts from birth family members, and these can be included with significant new items. Adding the first tooth that fell out or a swimming certificate can provide an opportunity to look again at earlier mementos. At some point in the future some of the bad memories can be integrated with the good ones.

## Important gaps

If your main experience of adoption has been through contact with people who adopted – or were adopted – many years ago, you are likely to have come across the idea of starting with a "clean sheet". Not only did adoption sever the legal tie with birth parents, but also the emphasis was on confirming the child's sense of belonging in their new family. Families did not necessarily receive many details about birth parents – especially letters – and the idea of tracing origins was not common. There are still many adults who were adopted who have no desire to find out more about their birth family, but of course there are others who do.

Being claimed within your adoptive family is very positive for children and their adoptive family, including all the relatives. For many children and their parents, there are mixed feelings about how far to go in seeking further information or opening up possible contact with birth family members. This involves making choices. For a small group of children, however, these choices simply may not exist. For children who have been abandoned as babies, whether in the UK or overseas, there may be no possibility of finding information. You may have a few details about where a child was found and what they were wearing to personalise your child's story. These are, however, the very first memories about your child that you may be able to access. For people with little information we know that the smallest details mean a lot. It may or may not be possible to meet the person who found your child or first cared for him or her, usually in hospital. Even if you cannot do this directly, the temporary carer might have some memories of what they picked up at the time. Comments such as 'The T-shirt she was wrapped in made me think her mother was very young'; 'It was such a busy area – his mother must have made a big effort to be sure he would be found quickly', or simply 'Despite the circumstances, that first cry showed me this one is a real survivor' all convey messages that could be very positive. In some cultures certain colours may be regarded as lucky and that may be recalled by whoever found your child.

At the same time, you need to think consciously about helping your child understand that certain options will not be open to them. Once children know they are adopted, they begin building up their picture of what that means. This includes information from other people and sources. They will need to know the reality of their situation before they build up hopes and expectations that cannot be realised. Your understanding of the sadness of that unfillable gap will be vital. Adopters are frequently good problem-solvers. Your child will need to learn both about ways to deal positively with challenges, and also how to live with what you cannot change.

---

Our daughter, adopted when she was seven, shies away from asking personal questions or referring to her life before she joined our family, and very often we have to look for opportunities to refer to her first six years. Because this was a time when she did not have a normal family life, she is often too anxious to blot out and forget these years. In an effort to help her sort out her very muddled memories and to fill in the gaps, we started to make a book. It took a good deal of persistence to get any relevant information from the social services department, and eventually I sent the social worker a long list of questions saying I would be grateful if only a few of them could be answered. I knew it was possible for him to visit her biological mother as she had been contacted in order to sign the consent form. I included all sorts of questions in the hope of gleaning information about her early babyhood and, considering the passage of time, I was grateful for the answers I received.

We then started slowly over many months to build her life story book. As writing was then a considerable labour for her, I did most of the simple factual writing, leaving her to put in the important information such as the date of her birth, where she was born, her first name, etc. We were able to illustrate the book with pictures and maps of the place of her birth, and we were fortunate in being able to obtain some photographs through various social workers and house-parents. Working on the book has given us both a wonderful opportunity to deepen our relationship in discussing a very intimate part of herself.

## Thoughts and feelings

*A significant event came when we were writing my daughter's life story. She wrote: 'I always thought it was my fault I was taken away,' something she had never voiced but felt able to write and subsequently to talk about. She was then able to accept that circumstances beyond her control, and beyond the control of her parents, had caused it all to happen. Harder things to face such as sexual abuse have also been best dealt with initially through the medium of the life story book leading to discussions on a personal level; the action of writing unpleasant things allowing a more detached way in. She has even said, 'Oh dear, I knew I would have to write this awful part one day'. But she has faced up to it and seems relieved to have done so. When I suggested that some day she might want to destroy the unpleasant parts of her book she said, 'Oh no, I couldn't do that, it's part of my life'. So now when she wants to share her book with someone, the difficult pages are temporarily removed and only left in for a handful of very trusted people.*

*It's important to be open and honest…If you think a child won't be able to understand their past – you're wrong. James understands who he is, which is vital to his self-esteem.*
From 'Knowing who you are', in *Could you be my Parent?* (Sturge-Moore (ed), 2005)

# 06

# The place of contact

*We always had a very positive attitude towards adoption, but there was something missing until we got the opportunity to write once a year to our daughter's birth mother. We now know that she receives our letters and photographs, that she appreciates them and that she is happy with the situation. I think I understand better now about the missing piece of a child's life if she has no information about her birth parents or the circumstances surrounding her birth and*

*subsequent adoption. I, too, felt it . . . there was a*
*person out there somewhere who had given life to*
*our precious daughter. I wanted to know more*
*about her, to feel that I shared something with*
*someone who thought and felt and was a real*
*person, not just a name.*

---

Alongside the move to much greater openness in adoption has
come the reality of some level of contact with birth family members.
Various research studies have identified some type of contact in well
over half of adoptive placements now. This opens up many more
options in talking about adoption. It provides both more access to
information, and also opportunities to initiate communication with
children or respond to their questions and concerns. Adopters often
worry about face-to-face contact or struggle to understand how it
could help their child, seeing it more as a reassurance to the birth
parents. This is particularly so with young children who have little or
no experience of living with their birth parents. It seems to make
more sense for older children who are distressed by the thought of
losing all contact with some members of their birth family. Yet the
research suggests that younger children may find it easier to take
contact in their stride as they do not have the same level of mixed
feelings about what has happened. During preparation to adopt you
probably looked at the long-term reasons for considering some level
of contact and thought about the purposes of this. As you think
about talking to your child about their adoption, you will be able to
reflect on the part contact might play in helping you do this. The
actual contact itself is only one part of how you might go about it
so it is really important to think about all that goes before and after.
How you judge contact also relates to the overall understanding of
your child and the effects of contact at different ages and stages.
Some degree of anxiety is natural and should be seen as part of
your child's development, but if there is evidence of overwhelming
upset then a break may be indicated.

Contact may be with birth parents, siblings, other relatives and
former foster carers and it may take many different forms.

Obviously, part of considering the initial link between you and your child will have included discussion of any contact arrangements which were thought to be in your child's interests. These can, however, change over time. There is now a growing amount of information both from children and from adoptive parents about how such contact works and how it fits in with children's understanding of their adoption. You will find this both in research studies and in personal stories. In looking for a practical framework for sorting out the potential value in some form of contact and also guidance on managing different types of arrangements you could look at BAAF's guide, *10 Top Tips for Managing Contact* (2007). This also includes some ideas on the newer ways in which contact can be maintained, such as through the use of mobile phones and email.

## Contact and intercountry adoption

Intercountry adopters often feel that contact has no relevance for them and may feel comfortable with the fact that their chosen route means that it will probably not take place. While this may be so in many cases, it is not true in every situation and global means of communication are increasingly opening up new possibilities – as are changing attitudes in some of the countries who need overseas adopters for their children. There are examples of "orphanages" in South American countries which try to keep in touch after children have been adopted overseas and can provide both a channel for further support in making sense of the need for adoption and potentially further information on both a child's birth family and also their early care.

Some families who became involved with children in other countries through aid activities and subsequently adopted a child may also have a link with other birth family members who are continuing to struggle in adverse circumstances. The adopted child may have been one too many for a destitute birth family to care for. Keeping a link open may have tremendous potential in helping a child understand the circumstances leading to adoption. At the same time, knowing about further challenges they continue to face can raise lots of feelings and dilemmas about how much you can also offer some further aid to them in your child's country of origin. While you can ask for advice from the UK adoption support services, it may be helpful to supplement this by contacting one of the organisations which focus on intercountry adoption (see Useful Organisations). If you completed your adoption some years ago and new questions are emerging, you may also find it useful to look at some of the more recent websites on intercountry adoption as a route to renewing knowledge and possibly even contact with your child's country. It is interesting to note that with the changes in legislation in England and Wales about the use of intermediaries, the Intercountry Adoption Centre now has an intermediary service for adoptions with an overseas element.

## Contact with birth parents

Contact with birth parents, and usually the birth mother in particular, is likely to be most emotive both for children and their adoptive parents. This may be an initial meeting with the birth parents (see Chapter 2), an arrangement for indirect exchange of information (often called a letterbox arrangement) or ongoing face-to-face or other direct contact such as telephone calls.

### Indirect contact

Such arrangements, often called "letterbox contact", are frequently set up when children are very young. The idea seems very simple but in practice can lead to many questions.

Although it is sometimes also called an "information exchange", the flow of information may be uneven. Some adopters will start enthusiastically writing about their child's progress for the birth parent but begin to question the purpose if there is no return flow. Do you then involve your child as she or he grows older if there is no two-way exchange? Is it really helping your child understand his or her origins and playing a part in talking about adoption?

You need to be clear at the outset how the contact has been explained to the birth parent and what can realistically be expected. Some birth parents may see the purpose as being primarily about letting them know about the child's development. If you are hoping for a reply which will help you in talking to your child, you need to think about what will increase the likelihood of that. If you have the chance to meet the birth parent, you may be able to explain your hopes. Some simple questions may come up both at the initial meeting and in the years following it that would be useful to check with the birth parent, such as whether a family member had a particular talent for dancing, big feet, etc! The early years are the time to establish such communication, to build up the picture for your child and let the birth parent see how they can help. You also need to know what arrangements there might be for screening information and how any significant changes in a birth parent's circumstances might be conveyed to you.

Clearly, once your child is old enough, she or he will need to be involved in the arrangement, perhaps choosing a photograph or suggesting what goes in a letter. By that stage, you are likely to have tested out whether a reply could be expected. If not, you could suggest to your child that you are sending information to the agency to keep safe in case the birth parent asks the agency how they are getting on.

In the long run, your child will have a view about whether they want to continue with such an arrangement, stop it or perhaps extend it to more direct contact. Children can be very sensitive to the feelings of their adoptive parents so this could be a point when she or he would benefit from either talking to a trusted member of the extended family, or a professional with a more objective position. If, on the other hand, there is no reply from the birth parent, it appears to be a non-issue with your child or she or he has lost interest in the contact, it is likely to be useful to round it off by writing to the adoption agency explaining the position and giving pointers to what would be possible if there is a change of mind in the future.

## Direct contact

This would normally only be arranged if the birth parents were either co-operating with the adoption, or were not likely to undermine your position as adoptive parents. Meetings rarely occur more frequently than three or four times a year. If you are involved in such an arrangement, you will know at the outset why such plans are seen as being in the best interests of your child.

Such a live link inevitably creates the necessity to talk about the adoption and the birth family. Arrangements need to be made; you will be picking up your child's anticipation and any apprehension; and new pieces of information about the birth family will be added to you and your child's knowledge.

Some adoptive parents who approached such arrangements with caution or even trepidation have found that, once they settled down, this proved the most natural way to keep a link open and integrate their child's knowledge of the past with their present understanding. Most of these arrangements are voluntary, so there is space for negotiation and evaluation of details as the child's needs change, and adoption support services take account of this. Most adopters look to their agency to arrange and monitor contact arrangements at the outset. In the long term this can continue through the adoption support plan, unless you feel that handling it yourself works better and is more flexible. If difficulties arise you can always return to seek further advice.

In more complex situations you may have started off with a direct contact arrangement in the short term which may or may not be expected to continue. This can occur where children move to potential adopters on a fostering basis in a contested situation before this has been resolved at court, temporary foster carers are adopting, or adopters have been involved in a concurrent planning project. Two key points to consider here are about your part in the original contact arrangements and how you explain to your child any change linked to the adoption plan. The nature and purpose of adoption is about providing the security that children need. Even if the long-term plan is that direct contact is not seen as best or necessary for a child, an interim arrangement is still part of

your child's experience in your family. Being there for him or her at
the time of contact gives a strong message about offering support
at such times. Even if a child is used to being collected from a
former foster home for contact at a familiar family centre, they need
to experience a permanent adoption placement as a different
situation – and this means they need to learn your strengths as
parents. In some situations you may be advised against actually
taking part in a contact meeting but could take your child, wait and
be there immediately afterwards. Some "short-term" arrangements
may continue for many months. If contact has happened regularly
during your initial relationship with your child you need to be able
to explain why it needs to stop with the granting of an adoption
order. Will the explanation make sense to the child? Is it clearly
rooted in her or his best interests? Would it be better to reduce the
frequency and then consider any further changes over the years
ahead depending on how your child is reacting, his or her views and
whether the birth parents can sustain it helpfully?

## Other relatives and foster carers

In the next chapter, we will consider brothers and sisters in more
detail. For adopted adults seeking members of their birth family,
they feature highly. This is not surprising given that our relationships
with our siblings are likely to be the longest lasting in our lives, even
if there are periods when we don't see so much of them. In
planning for adoption, grandparents frequently feature as an option
either for caring for children or supporting the birth parents. For
older children, they may have offered direct care at some point,
even if they were unable to offer long-term care. Older children may
also have memories of time spent with aunts and uncles or cousins.

'Children can hold two families in their hearts and minds
without suffering conflicts of loyalty - if the situation is
managed carefully. After all, most of us have two sets of

grandparents , and possibly several aunts and uncles, cousins, nieces and nephews. We may have a very strong attachment to a particular cousin we only see at major family occasions, or hold fond memories of an uncle who emigrated to Australia when we were very young. We accept, quite naturally, that there are a finite number of people in our everyday lives and a whole world of other people who are important to us, but only encountered at certain times.

However, if we knew we would never see or hear from our favourite cousin or our Australian uncle again, we would probably begin a process of mourning; which is what happens to children who believe they will never encounter their birth relatives again.

From *Ten Top Tips for Managing Contact* (Bond, 2007)

---

For other children, their clearest memories from before they joined you will be of activities in their foster home – outings, holidays, school plays and family activities. Most people can recall the pleasure of occasional reminiscing and the re-telling of old stories, especially if you've moved to a new area.

For children who have experienced many moves, a sense of continuity needs to be actively encouraged. If parts of your life and the people in it can disappear, what sense do words like "forever" make? The introductory period and the early stages of placement are the best time to lay the foundations of the future contacts that may be used positively for your child. Some contact may also bring some sadness – reminders of losses, triggers for difficult memories as well as good ones. At the same time, in sharing these earlier times with your child, you will be demonstrating acceptance of the earlier life experiences he or she has brought into your family. Foster carers and relatives who are in favour of your child's adoption can extend both your own and your child's understanding of past events and also help with the recurring question, 'Why was I adopted?'

**USEFUL RESOURCES WHICH EXPLORE CONTACT**

Several books on contact are listed in Useful Books.
Additionally, two useful videos have been produced by
Families Are Best, Catholic Children's Society, Nottingham,
about contact, titled *Contact in Adoption*. The first gives the
experiences of adoptive parents whose children have some
form of contact with birth family members, and the second
gives the views of some children and young people.

**Thoughts and feelings**

*Re: birth mother: 'I only see her when I feel
comfortable about seeing her. She's nice, she's got
problems…but I do see her.'*

*Re: birth father: 'But if he's changed and be nice,
be really good and sensible then I would be able to
contact…but if he's not then I wouldn't.'*

*Re: foster carers: 'I think it's quite good to keep in*

*contact because when we were younger, we
didn't, like, know much about them and, like, how
they looked after us when we were younger, what
they did for us while we were there.*
From *Adopted Children Speaking* (Thomas and
Beckford, 1999)

---

*It doesn't upset me to send the letter...I wonder
what other parent would sit down and do this? To
write about your child's achievements over a year is
so unusual, but so amazing.*
From 'Wondering what to write', in *Could you be
my Parent?* (Sturge-Moore (ed), 2005)

---

# 07

# Brothers and sisters

*…my brother Michael, he's living in [nearby district], he's adopted there. Not five minutes away over the fields and we don't know where…I think I bumped into him once. Well, it looked like him. I don't know whether it was or not…*
From *We are Family* (Mullender (ed), 1999)

So far this book has referred to "your child", which recognises that each child is an individual developing his or her unique understanding of being adopted. But in thinking of children joining adoptive families, their relationships with brothers and sisters is a vast and diverse area. In *We are Family* (Mullender (ed), 1999), various writers explored sibling relationships in adoptive and foster placements with all sorts of charts and definitions of full, half- and step-siblings brought up together or apart. Statistics of children placed for adoption show that a high number are placed together with at least one full or half-sibling. Evidence from children in foster care also shows how much they know about the wide number of other siblings elsewhere in their networks, for example, knowing that their birth father had other children living somewhere else. Most children in foster care have siblings – whether or not they are placed with them or will move to adoption with them. The birth parents of babies placed for adoption often go on to have more children. Then, in moving into an adoptive family, many children acquire new siblings through adoption. Handling the myriad of issues that come up with siblings is likely both to highlight your own views and values about brothers and sisters and also to challenge your skills in managing sibling interactions.

## Those who are together

Many families who come to adoption because of infertility issues hope ultimately to have more than one child. If each child joins the family as a baby, like any family the initial emphasis is about welcoming the newcomer and helping the bigger brothers or sisters adjust to the demands of a younger sibling. Adoptive families often use this time to recall with older children how they joined the family. At such times, it is useful to have photographs of earlier first meetings to look at alongside current introductions. Learning to share and having consideration and concern for other family members is all part of growing up for children. The added dimension of adoption can be a positive factor in such learning.

Children who are adopted need a clear sense of belonging and an understanding that legally they are part of their adoptive family, while learning about their different biological families. The increasingly diverse reasons why children are placed for adoption and all the developments in understanding genetics can complicate the picture. Two children in any family may have very different personalities, needs and interest in their origins. For adopted children, they may also have very different histories, so talking to them individually and as a family needs to take this into account.

From an early stage, you need to think about family guidelines on what is shared and what is kept private. One child, for example, may be involved in a contact arrangement, which the other does not have. You may want to include the child in deciding how much detail they share with a brother or sister, but the basic differences in arrangements will be clear and need to be acknowledged. This is likely to change over time, as will your knowledge of your children and what works for them and for you all as a family. Family discussions may be a feature of your lifestyle and approach, or your emphasis may be on making space for individual time for each child. Sharing a common bond through adoption into your family may be very comforting for your children, but individuals may vary in their need for separate personal space.

Even babies now may be adopted with information about siblings placed elsewhere. If another child is born into the birth family of one of your children, you may well be contacted with that information. This may open up discussions about who is your brother or sister and why your children may have different numbers of siblings! Formal family trees do not usually work for such complex networks, but there are now more ideas around for helping children visualise who is connected to them. The simplest is probably a drawing of a tree with leaves for significant people, including both birth and adoptive family and perhaps close friends or previous carers. For siblings this can provide a way to think about who they share in common alongside important links for themselves as individuals.

Other adopters hoping for more than one child actively seek to adopt a sibling group of two or more children. Many of these children are also older and may have lived with their birth family for a while. From your point of view as an adoptive parent, this has potential advantages. The children share a joint history and any contact arrangements may be shared also. If your child or children are already familiar with the *Nutmeg* stories, there are a number of themes there relevant to siblings both as a group placed together, and then with the addition of a new baby sister. An older child may be able to help a younger one understand the reasons for their adoption.

However, it may not always be quite so simple in reality! From the beginning, one child may be more prepared or eager for a move and be more willing to share feelings and experiences openly. One child may want and need contact that seems meaningless or is resisted by the other. An older child may come out with graphic details of earlier experiences that a younger one may not be ready to hear. A pattern of sibling relationships may have been established that you hope to change, for example, an older child taking too much responsibility for a younger sibling. Siblings may have been viewed differently in the birth family – one might have been a favoured child or another the scapegoat. This may be linked to areas like gender; whether the family was coping or in the middle of crisis when a particular child was born; or different views of birth fathers if you have adopted half-siblings. Where there are half-siblings, one child may have a lot of knowledge of their birth father and his extended family and another may have none. This can be even more complicated if one birth father is of a different ethnic origin to another.

You should of course know about such issues in advance, as they should have been part of the assessment of whether a particular group of siblings need to be placed together or separately. The more you get to grips with all these possible dimensions at the outset, the better prepared you will be both for day-to-day parenting of your children together and also all the issues that could come up in talking about adoption.

Within an adoptive family, not all children may have joined by that route. There are some families which include birth children who themselves may be full or half-siblings, adopted children and perhaps also foster children. This is where the concept of different ways to join a family is useful. Children need to learn that within your family everyone is valued as an individual and needs their own space and "special" time, but that no one is always more "important" than everyone else. This is also where the idea of an adopted child being specially chosen is most likely to be unhelpful! Some advance preparation with grandparents and other relatives may reap benefits. They need to understand how you view building your family. The question of "favourites" can come up in every family, and often relatives are already aware of the pitfalls of this if they appear to share a special interest with one grandchild or niece. The added implications of how this could be interpreted by an adopted child need to be considered. This does not mean to say that everyone has to ensure that all the children in the family are treated the same way all the time. What it does mean is that you need to think consciously about how you handle times when one child needs more attention, and how you explain to your children separately and as a family group if one child's needs must come first at a particular time.

Relatives and friends can be very useful here in helping with other children. Your adopted child may have a contact outing with birth family members, so activities for other family members may be welcomed. The frequency of such events will dictate whether there is a risk of creating a split between an adopted child and a birth child. Clearly, such events will be within the context of plenty of shared family time. Where tensions arise between siblings, families will have their own repertoire of ways of handling them, often based on childhood experiences. With a "mixed" family of birth and adopted children, some added reassurances may be needed to confirm everyone's place in the family. Your knowledge of each of your children's abilities, personalities and aptitudes should provide you with ways of highlighting their role and place in the family, for example, he's the joker or she's the one we rely on to feed the fish!

Where an adopted child joins a family, which includes birth children, while still a baby, the usual range of big sister/brother responses are likely. It is often only much later that the questions both from the adopted child and the birth child arise. Earlier chapters have covered dealing with these with your adopted child. Some similar discussions may need to happen with birth children who may equally hear comments from others or be questioned at school. Just as you may have needed to explain to an adopted child about what is private information, so you need to help your birth children understand the same boundaries from a different perspective. You may also want to give them ideas about what to do if an adopted brother or sister chooses to confide in them about something worrying or to use them as a channel of communication.

This particular aspect may come up more quickly with children who are older when placed. This book cannot cover all the scenarios that arise in moving from preparing children for a new sibling joining them by adoption to experiencing the reality. Efforts to be the welcoming older sibling may be rejected or a more sheltered child may be shocked and distressed by revelations of experiences way beyond the drama in *Harry Potter* or *Paddington Bear*. This is increasingly recognised in projects for birth children in families who foster. Some families may find videos like *Children who Foster*, the CD-ROM *Bridget's Taking a Long Time,* the DVD/video *Just a Member of the Family*, or the book *We are Fostering* (see Useful Books) are relevant for them too during preparation, while others may like to try linking with other "mixed" families.

## Those who are separated

A growing number of adopters now bring children into their family knowing they have siblings elsewhere. If you are in this position, how you handle talking about it in the years ahead will be influenced by the age of your child when he or she joined your family, the reasons for their separate placement from siblings, where these siblings are living and whether there is any contact.

Very young children may have been separated from their siblings early on or may never have lived with them, and therefore may have little or no direct relationship. Many adopters have a belief in the importance of sibling relationships which will influence them in sharing information and looking for the potential to meet. Helping your child understand about his or her siblings will be just one dimension, albeit an important one, of building up his or her understanding of adoption and knowledge of individual circumstances. You will need to feel confident about the reasons why your child is being adopted separately from his or her siblings.

For older children who have lived with their siblings, especially where there has been a deliberate decision to seek separate placements, there will be important relationships to consider as well as picking up on explanations that your child may be struggling to understand. Finding out about the assessments and professional discussions that led to the split for your child needs to be supplemented by finding out from carers if that has made any sense to the child! It is, for example, much easier to explain that an older half-sibling has been with a paternal grandparent for years than to say why your child is the only one not at home with their birth mother, or why two children who know their foster carers struggled to manage them together are now going in different directions. Being "good" or "bad" can be a worry for a lot of children who have been adopted, especially if they have moved around different foster homes. Adoptive parents of brothers or sisters often come across the "see-saw" effect. One adoptive parent said, 'I did realise that part of what was going on was that the one who was not in trouble was in fact behaving well in order to try and hold the placement together for himself and also his brother. It was as if the "good" one could not risk behaving badly while his brother acted out, through fear of us not being able to cope – and ending the placement.'

If, however, a split happens, not only may children carry a belief that they have been "bad" but also, if they have tried to be "good", they can feel guilty that they have failed or feel that they are just not good enough.

At the time when separations happen, children usually feel confused or vulnerable. Explanations given may be half heard or not really believed. It can take many years for children to build up a real understanding of such times in their lives. Your child may be able to repeat some of the explanations given to her or him, but can only express some of their anxieties much later when they feel secure and have built up their self-confidence.

You may therefore find that a child who seemed to have accepted a split from a brother or sister quite well may at a later stage start to question more. Keeping up any contact arrangements may feel more difficult at some times if your child is facing fresh questions which she or he was not ready to ask before. While in the long run this is progress, it may not feel like that at the time. Equally, meeting up with siblings can re-awaken thoughts about the rest of the birth family. Knowing about siblings and hearing of their progress can be immensely reassuring for children who are separated and is often a happy occasion with a lot of fun. It can also bring up more unsettling feelings and questions. Listening to your child at these times and showing them you accept and understand the tough bits can help bring you closer. For many young people, the sadness of not seeing siblings who are elsewhere can be longer lasting than the upset that may be triggered by a meeting which stirs up memories.

And finally...some families are juggling all the aspects of building relationships between children who have joined their family in different ways, thus creating sibling relationships, while acknowledging that some of their children are also separated from siblings placed elsewhere. While this can seem a tall order, families who are good at valuing and nurturing relationships between their children are well placed to be sensitive to worries about brothers or sisters elsewhere. Frequent contact may not be realistic or advisable, but in a society where many children have contact with separated parents or half-siblings growing up somewhere else, such arrangements in adoption situations are not unique.

## Thoughts and feelings

*Clearly siblings will have a shared past and we rather naively hoped that being placed together would help the boys in terms of dealing with the impact of past losses in their lives, especially the deaths of their mother and grandmother…*
*However, Karl and Arron had experienced the losses of the past differently and even to the present day (with both of them now adults), they have not actually been able to help each other.*
*I would say, however, that growing up in a family with several adopted children, and being part of a social network with other adoptive families, has helped all of them deal better with being adopted, and has lessened the feeling that it must somehow be their fault.*

*When I came into care there was me and my two brothers and my little sister…She was only about six months old the last time I saw her.*
From Harrison in *We are Family* (Mullender (ed), 1999)

*I do miss him. Sometimes I get desperate to see him…I used to get desperate to see him when I left him and sometimes it's quite upsetting, but I don't get that as much. I don't get that now…I do look forward to seeing him, but I don't, like, get desperate. I get used to it.*
Girl who speaks to brother on phone and sees him about three times a year. They have been apart for six years.
From *Adopted Children Speaking* (Thomas and Beckford, 1999)

*I like him, 'cause I mean, if you see your sister or brother too much then you end up arguing sometimes, don't you? If you only see them a few times, like twice a month or something, then you get on with them.*
*Boy who has a brother in another adoptive family nearby.*
From *Adopted Children Speaking* (Thomas and Beckford, 1999)

# 08

# Foster carers who adopt

*I was wanting to be adopted but it was just really the same. I mean it didn't change anything – yet if I had not been adopted, I would have been quite disappointed because by law, I wouldn't be here.*
From Triseliotis and Hill in *The Psychology of Adoption* (Brodzinsky and Schechter (eds), 1993)

If your starting point was a wish to adopt, your preparation and assessment will have been geared to lifetime issues and the questions raised for adopted children and adults, about their need for knowledge of their history and why they were adopted. If, however, you were approved as a foster carer, your preparation will have had a different emphasis because normally at the start of any placement, a return to birth parents is the first consideration.

When permanent plans are made for children now, an increasing number of foster carers are choosing or are encouraged to change their focus and become a child's permanent family. Some local authorities now calculate that about a third of their school-aged children who cannot return home remain with their "temporary" carers who are then recognised as their new family. For children who have struggled through various moves and periods of uncertainty, there are clear advantages to this, and whilst not all of these children will be legally adopted, a significant number will. The introduction of special guardianship in England and Wales has provided another option for permanence for older children wanting security without being adopted, and some carers may feel more confident of ongoing support. In Scotland, the Permanence Order will also provide an alternative when it is implemented.

Even for very young children there can be delays in sorting out the best long-term plan. Attachments can easily be formed between foster carers and children placed with them as babies. Our understanding now of early attachments and the effect of moves on young children means that for babies and young children also, adoption by their temporary foster carers may be the best plan.

## Relationships with birth parents

Regardless of the age of the child when the plan is made, there are some aspects of talking about adoption that are specific to foster carers who adopt. One of the most important of these is the likelihood of a relationship at the outset with the birth parent(s). In talking about adoption and their birth family's circumstances to their child, many adopters rely on information and reports from social workers. Some have the opportunity for a face-to-face meeting, but normally adopters would not have had any prolonged contact with the birth family members. Foster carers, on the other hand, may have spent a lot of time trying to help a parent care for a child before the adoption plan was made. Sometimes birth parents will tell foster carers more than they tell social workers. Some very needy birth parents may enjoy contact visits as much for time spent with the foster carers as with their child. Foster carers therefore often have a "head start" in knowing some of the day-to-day stories and anecdotes about birth family members. If you are in that position, it is useful to gather together any photographs or mementos of any events or outings that were shared in this way. Even if some continuing contact post-adoption is agreed, it is likely to be less frequent and may fall away.

Of course, not all your direct knowledge of birth family members is likely to be positive. It is important when you are considering adopting a child whom you have fostered to be honest about your views of his or her birth parents. Many birth parents are unhappy individuals who have had more than their fair share of problems, or have significant gaps in their abilities. Your personal link with a particular child's birth parent may be invaluable in helping you give your child a rounded and compassionate understanding of why they could not return home.

Sometimes, however, foster carers are left struggling with distressed children who have been let down by birth parents, may have seen parents at their worst and in some cases even been threatened by them. If you are caught up in the middle of events which are damaging for children, it is hard to avoid some feelings of anger or frustration. You may also feel very let down if a planned rehabilitation started well then fell apart. Unlike adopters with no personal involvement with a child's background and history, you may sometimes feel you have too much!

This is when it is helpful to use some social work support to look as objectively as possible at your feelings about what has happened so far. Your relationship with your child's birth parents may have changed during the making of the adoption plan. Some earlier good times may be affected by their anger if they see you as part of "losing" their child or having very reduced contact. If you have tried hard together to develop a birth mother's parenting skills, you may be very aware of her sadness and distress if this is still not enough for the child's welfare. Sometimes, birth parents can be relieved if their child is to be adopted by known foster carers. They may be able to tell the child this. Whatever the circumstances and however it happened, this is all a vital part of the explanation to the child that will be built on over the years.

## Differences between fostering and adoption

In Chapter 2, there was discussion of the information adopters might need to answer a child's questions. It is important for foster carers also to ensure that they have drawn all this information together. Sometimes foster carers gather their knowledge of a child and his or her history in a more piecemeal way over time. This is rather different from the comprehensive "package" that should accompany children into an adoptive placement. This is where it is useful to take stock and check out any assumptions that might have been made. There is some anecdotal evidence of foster carers who were quite happy at the time of the adoption but who later discover some gaps in what they have to share with their child, or find that the background information is not in a child-friendly or cohesive form.

Reference has already been made to different preparations for adoption and for fostering. If you are moving from one type of care to another, you need to pick up on some of these differences and make sure that, on top of all your fostering skills and experience, you have had space to look at the specific tasks involved in adoption. Some agencies run groups for foster carers who are "converting" to adoption.

No matter how this happens in your agency, your whole family needs to understand the differences. Many families who foster already include birth children. In addition, you might also be caring for older children who are likely to remain but **not** be adopted. Sometimes, families intend to continue short-term fostering as well.

In day-to-day living there will be no dramatic change or a move to consider, but there may be subtle changes in relationships. More importantly, over time questions may arise about why children are in the family in different ways. The child who has been adopted, birth children and other foster children may all need more discussion of this at different times. Useful opportunities for confirming a child's place in the family or picking up traces of anxieties can often come up naturally in family life in homes which are flexible in including children in different ways.

If your family has been fostering for a long time, you are likely to be used to talking to children about their birth parents and the difficult circumstances surrounding them. The big change is in the legal status. For many adopted children, the court hearing is a significant landmark. Not going back home and needing reassurance of where they will be for the remainder of their childhood is highly important for many children and young people in foster care. The child you are adopting will ultimately need to understand why the plan for them included the severance of their legal relationship with their birth parents and the transfer of those lifelong responsibilities to you. Unlike those who set out to adopt, this was not your original intention, so you do need to be clear about the reasons for the plan, alongside the emotional attachments formed between you and the child.

It is interesting to note that some research suggests that children in foster care are far more likely to have met other foster children, than they are to have met adopted children. Teenagers in foster care may be quite clear that they will stay where they are until they are independent but don't want to change their name or lose their legal link with their birth family. You need to be clear whether you or they can share this distinction helpfully with a younger child you plan to adopt. Some of the thoughts and ideas covered in earlier chapters about legal status, confidentiality and sibling relationships are relevant here.

Older children will be familiar with social workers and reviews, so practical changes in this are useful markers of their altered status. If you continue to foster they may well be reminded of this. While as adults we may be wary of comparisons that might be reassuring to one child but unsettling to another, children do inevitably pick up a lot from others who may be in similar situations. A child you adopted earlier may make sense of the stages she or he went through in being aware of the options being debated for other children. It is intriguing to note in some research that, alongside the negative stories we sometimes hear about children from damaging backgrounds, there is a more encouraging side as well. Many young adults who had very uncertain periods in their lives end up, for example, in the caring professions. Support in handling adverse background factors helps many children build resilience and compassion for others. As children in this position get older, they may gain confidence and self-esteem in understanding and helping others who are more vulnerable.

Timescales at certain points are often less pressurised if children are remaining with their foster carers. Foster carers preparing children to move on to adopters can find that sometimes a placement is found while the child is still struggling to understand the plan. At other times, a child is ready to move and then there is an agonising wait. Some of the children who contributed to *Adopted Children Speaking* (Thomas and Beckford, 1999) and were adopted by their foster carers were far less likely to be worried about the plan. Instead, as foster carers you will need to think about how much space to give your particular child in choosing to be adopted. The age of your child and his or her ability to cope with choices will guide you once the plan is being finalised. Some children respond well to active involvement in the different stages, while others are reassured by the confidence of others in making the best plan for their future. For many children, therefore, the tone will be set by the social workers involved as well as by you and also the responsibility your agency is taking for the decisions made.

If your child's birth parents are still in touch, their views over the planning period will also be significant in thinking about the ongoing explanations. Some birth parents, given time and their knowledge of the care the child has received so far, may be able to be "positive" in what they say.

On the other hand, the agency and the social workers may need to take the brunt of a birth parent's anger at losing their child, and the child may need to know just how the decision was made.

Talking about the plan for adoption, therefore, is likely to be a shared task for quite a period. The quality of the work with your child at this stage before formal adoption will lay solid foundations for the years ahead. One piece of research, *The Psychology of Adoption* (Brodzinsky and Schechter, 1993), explains: 'It was not as if suddenly these children and young people felt different or transformed or things changed for them. Rather, they gradually became aware of a change in status that conveyed intangible feelings of "belonging" and being the family's "real child", which was unlike fostering…'

## Adopting babies or toddlers

So far, the emphasis in this chapter has been on foster carers adopting children who are old enough to be included in some way in knowing about the adoption plan. Sometimes, however, all this planning and the adoption itself may have happened when your child was still at the pre-verbal stage. You may have fostered this child almost from birth and in many ways you are in a similar position to other adopters of young children. Much in the earlier chapters about starting to talk to young children applies. Joining in with some of the preparation or support groups for adoptive parents is likely to be helpful both in tuning into adoption issues, and also perhaps in making links for your child with other adopted children.

The much more open approach to adoption now means that the earlier push to have a complete break between the temporary carers, where birth parents could visit, and the adoptive home is less of an issue. Even so, in most situations of relinquished babies, young children usually move from temporary carers to fully prepared and approved adopters quite quickly, hopefully before they are six months old. If babies wait significantly longer to be settled with their adoptive families, there are likely to be additional factors that may have implications in the years ahead for their adoption story. Few foster carers now only offer pre-adoption fostering, so caring for a newborn baby may be a new fostering experience for many carers. Inevitably bonds and attachments grow, especially if a baby needs extra care and attention. It is important, therefore, that the long-term adoption issues are addressed honestly at the outset when you are grappling with all the emotions around a potential separation from a much-loved baby. Some things to think about include the points below.

Delay may have been caused by the birth parents' ambivalence or difficulty in sorting out their problems. The placement may have been deliberately planned to test this out. If birth parents can acknowledge the care you have given to the child and the relationship formed, this can enable you to talk to your child positively about why staying with you was best. However, if birth parents oppose the plan, you need to think about what may be noted in the adoption records about why this particular plan was in your child's best interests. Unlike new adopters, you are not coming in once the plan is finally agreed and therefore independent from that decision. Your views of the situation are likely to have formed a part of the decision. You may even have had to give evidence against the birth parents. It will help you in the future if there is a clear explanation on record for your child of the reasons why they remained with you despite their birth parent's views. Normally this is about the plan rather than personal to you.

Some babies stay longer because there are question marks about their development or they have clear medical problems. You may or may not have advance knowledge about children of parents who misused drugs or alcohol during pregnancy, very premature babies who are slow to develop or children with specific conditions like Down's syndrome or cerebral palsy. Caring for the child while the medical picture is built up gives you a chance to know the whole child.

Sometimes the reason for a child's extra challenges is one of the difficult parts of the explanation of adoption. All adopters struggle to find ways to deal with parental lifestyles or actions that affected their children or caused damage by abuse. As your child's former foster carer, when the time comes you will be able to talk not just about knowing his or her extra needs when you chose to adopt him or her, but also your knowledge of his or her parents and the adults' needs too.

The decision may not have been straightforward. Temporary fostering placements do not initially take account of all the long-term considerations. It may not have been possible to keep a child with older brothers or sisters, or find a fostering placement that reflected the child's ethnicity, religion or culture. You may be older than the age normally considered by your agency for adopters of babies or young children. Once the adoption plan is made, questions about keeping siblings together or taking into account the child's heritage inevitably come to the fore again. Your agency will have had to think about the impact of a move for your child alongside these lifetime questions. Time – how long to look for alternatives and how long the child has been with you – will become critical. If you have been through one of these situations, you will be very aware of how emotional a time it can be and the soul searching involved. There is inevitably relief once a conclusion is reached but as your child grows up and starts asking questions, you will need to be able to deal with these dilemmas openly. Demonstrating to your child that you took all aspects of her or his needs seriously is the best starting point. This means putting in place strategies from the start for dealing with areas where you may not have been the "ideal" match. For example, maintaining sibling contact or developing your knowledge and links with your child's cultural heritage require solid planning.

If you stop fostering soon after adopting a small child, your child, like most children in the community, will not automatically be aware of how decisions are made. As time passes, she or he may need to go beyond knowing how much you loved him or her, the importance of the bonds formed and your shared history together. It may also be useful for him or her to know that it was not only your choice but that other people were involved. You will be able to talk both about the steps taken by the agency, including the adoption panel decisions, and also about the Children's Guardian, or curator *ad litem* in Scotland, and the court's consideration. All these will confirm how seriously everything was considered, and how many people concluded it was best for your child to stay with you.

## Thoughts and feelings

*It meant quite a lot, because that meant I could stay with my mum [foster mother] when I wanted to.*
From *Adopted Children Speaking* (Thomas and Beckford, 1999)

*I wanted to go to court actually to watch everything being finalised…seeing like the case being closed…the book shut on it really…I love reading the ending of a book because of the feeling of triumph that you've finished it…and I guess that was the same feeling in court, watching them close the book, really shutting it…knowing that nothing else was going to happen. It was just going to be an ordinary life from now on…*

*Anne: I was fostered for two years and then I decided I wanted to get adopted and…*
*Interviewer: (interrupting) You decided?*
*Anne: Yeah. And then I was allowed to have the discussion whether or not to get adopted…and I really wanted to be adopted. Mum and Dad said it was up to me…*

# 09

# Respecting differences

*When I started school my mum had to talk to me quite a lot about my scars and skin colour because at break times we used to play games where you held hands in a circle and to start with some of the girls would not hold my hands because they didn't like the look of them. It helped me to come to terms with being scarred when my mum talked to me about the fire and how I spent five or six months in hospital being treated for burns.*

At the beginning of this book, we brought up the idea of thinking of adoption as one of the ways of children joining your family rather than highlighting that children are "different" because they are adopted. But, like any group of children, those who are adopted will have many other differences. There are lots of ways that children can be seen as different in school or in your local community. Some children may stand out because of their behaviour, others may have an impairment or a medical problem that means they cannot join in easily with some children's activities. Other children may be seen as different because they are black within a society which is largely white. Most of these children will be with their birth parents, some will be with relatives, step-parents or foster carers. You will all, as parents, have to think about ways to help your children feel good about themselves when people make thoughtless or unkind remarks.

Behind all this, of course, are issues of prejudice and stereotyping. These can affect both the birth parents and the child you adopt. Children growing up in the UK will frequently hear debates about topics like asylum seekers, Muslim fundamentalism or human rights violations in different parts of the world. Your child is also likely to become aware of different views of single parents, gay relationships, anti-social families and all the social issues that surround us. These can be in the media or amongst family and friends. As your child gets older and knows more of his or her background, she or he might pick up comments that strike a personal chord. Again, if you share your child's heritage or have direct experience of dealing with negative remarks that might be made, you will have worked out ways of deciding when to challenge these views and how to make sure there are clear, explicit positive messages around too.

Adoptive parents who do not share these direct experiences need to learn how to deal with them. It is tempting to be protective, especially if family and friends are very supportive and welcoming of your child. This is, of course, what you want as a good family experience for your child. However, it is with the love and support of your family that your child will need to learn about the realities of their wider community. They will also believe your comments about valuing their personal difference if you consistently challenge all types of discrimination and stereotyping.

## Your child's experience of difference

This book has made frequent reference to *Adopted Children Speaking* (Thomas and Beckford, 1999). The section in that research which explored children's experiences at school found that about half of the group of children interviewed did not want other children to know they were adopted. Approximately a third described being bullied at school. Most thought the bullying was directly related to other children's knowledge of them being adopted, or in some way "different". Of course, we know there are all sorts of reasons for bullying at school. What is a frequent theme, however, is that in some way, a particular child stands out. If the fact that your child is adopted has been picked out, you may need to liaise with the school about handling this, as well as returning to your child's worries about how being adopted is seen by others.

Giving your child answers for those who make thoughtless comments may be enough. Some children, however, have other areas of difference that are the focus of attention. These may be an integral part of their adoption and connections may be made. Your child may have difficulty concentrating, may have gaps in their knowledge of ordinary childhood experiences or be prone to occasional outbursts of difficult behaviour. Unhelpful comments may be made about what can be expected of adopted children or the background they come from.

There are now some useful leaflets around for schools to help them understand this from the adopters' and the child's point of view, and more joint training on the needs of children who are, or have been, in the care system. You may be able to make good use of the booklet *Welcoming Children into your Neighbourhood*, by Jane Espley, as part of increasing awareness in your community. Adopters' self-help groups, such as Adoption UK, are very aware of education issues and the benefits of providing information for schools. The

Intercountry Adoption Centre publishes some information on adoption and schools. In different parts of the UK, the needs of vulnerable children within education, including those in the care system, have been receiving attention. The various government websites can keep you up to date with the different reports being produced and suggested developments in services. Of course, many children who are not adopted also have problems at school and get into trouble. Your child will need a strong message from you that you understand what is going on, and this is something on which you can work together. You may be feeling anxious and uncertain, but this is when your child needs to see you as confident and committed to supporting her or him with whatever is troubling them.

Your child may have extra challenges in learning. Whether she or he goes to a special school or has classroom support, she or he may come to realise there are things that they cannot do that other children of their age can manage easily. Other children and adults may be very supportive and keen to include your child, but some people can be thoughtless and unpleasant, or exclude your child. Much of this is about other people's attitudes to disability and community views of children with impairments. Some adoptive parents find it very useful to be able to say, 'We knew all about you when we decided to adopt you'; other adopters may only learn over time that their child has a particular impairment. Joining self-help organisations can be a great help in adjusting your views of your child's future and finding out from other parents ways to help your child feel good about herself or himself.

Whether your child is at risk of negative comments at school because of behaviour or some impairment, they will need to have the same message of "unconditional love" as all children in secure families. For the adopted child, this is all the more important. Adopted children, especially at certain stages of development, may be particularly sensitive about the fact of no longer being with their birth families. Assurances about always being there for them may be harder for them to believe. Add to this fears about being different and it is not hard to imagine why a child may have anxieties about whether you really want them. Such fears are usually too scary to voice. While some children can respond by acting up, many others may disguise such worries by working hard to please you and their peers and by "protecting" you from being upset. This is where you need to be alert to a child who finds it hard to talk about any difference or denies the obvious. Schools or honest friends can help in alerting you to any discriminatory or negative experiences your child may be having but does not want to tell you about.

## The needs of black and minority ethnic children

In talking about different backgrounds, we have already looked at how adoptive parents need to understand their child's cultural heritage. This is important for the child's identity, their understanding of the context in which their adoption was planned and also the ramifications if they should have any contact with birth relatives or trace them in the future.

Your child's ethnicity will, at the same time, be a vital part of his or her whole childhood experience and day-to-day living. There are many adopters who do not fully share their child's heritage. In preparing them for adoption and considering possible links, attention will be paid both to their willingness to seek out information and to their demonstration of a family ethos which respects different lifestyles, beliefs and cultures.

Within the UK, we are sensitive to whether birth parents see themselves as English, Welsh, Scottish, or Irish; many white families have ancestors from different countries in Europe which are part of their identity. People from the Caribbean identify with specific islands; there are huge variations in African and Asian cultures, religions, and national identities. Intercountry adopters often become aware, too, that within certain countries, particular groups, such as Roma families, are discriminated against and these backgrounds feature more in the children placed for adoption.

Becoming more specific in these areas does not alter the reality that many children experience if they are visibly different in our society. If you are yourself from an identifiably different ethnic group, you are likely to have a store of experiences about this, either from your own experiences or through friends and relatives. You may not share your child's specific cultural background and will need to learn about this, but you will have an established basis for supporting your child in the face of racist comments. You may still have to respond to comments from your child or other people, that as parent and child you look different. The earlier comments about respecting and valuing difference will guide you in how you talk to your child, what you expect in the language and attitudes of your support network and your response to insensitive language and comments from others.

White adopters of black or minority ethnic children need to be especially aware of the potential for their child to be on the receiving end of unhelpful racist comments. "Colour" cannot be ignored. Generally, although young children may have limited understanding of words, they do begin to perceive differences and attach values to them. From observations of small children in playgrounds and nursery school, it is increasingly accepted that children are aware of different skin colour by about the age of two and at the age of three and four are rating such characteristics as more or less desirable. At this early age, your child will also be becoming aware if he or she is a different colour, or has very different features from you.

This is the crucial time to engage in open discussion of this difference. Your child is recognising that she or he is not just different from a number of the other children she or he mixes with outside the home, but also within the family. This is the time to acknowledge the differences your child is observing in as natural and relaxed a way as possible. Easy availability of books and toys which reflect children of all ethnicities helps. There is a temptation to think that not referring to a child's different ethnicity is demonstrating acceptance and indicating that it makes no difference. As adopters, you may hope you are showing acceptance that does not need to be put into words. You need to check that your child sees this in the same way and is not left feeling that their difference is something you are uncertain about raising. This needs to be balanced by a strong message about your child's place in your family and that "difference" does not affect their sense of belonging. Your child cannot feel comfortable about this if they also feel there are aspects that are central to themselves that they are not able to talk about easily.

---

Between 2004 and 2007, a study was carried out of intercountry adoption in Ireland. This looked at various aspects including the experiences of the children. Amongst the many findings, there are some of particular relevance to this subject.

The adopters who were least likely to respond to the researchers were the parents of teenagers – usually from Romania as this was the main country of origin for intercountry adoptions at the time.

Teachers and parents seemed relatively unaware of the kind of bullying experiences and negativity about adoption, "race" and ethnicity being experienced from time to time by the children who were interviewed. The study was careful not to overstate this and put it in the context of generally positive outcomes, but considered that parents were very capable of ignoring aspects of their children's experiences they did not want to recognise and children were motivated to protect their parents or avoid fuss and hassle.

At the interviews, many of the children had a desire for information which had not been met, probably because there was little to share.

The children's basic adoption story often seemed to become ritualised and frequently repeated. The interviews indicated that parents may be overestimating the level of their children's knowledge and understanding. Linked with this may be the finding that many of the children saw adoption in terms of being transferred from one country to another, rather than in terms of becoming the legal child of parents to whom they were not genetically related. The fact that birth relatives in intercountry adoption are often shadowy figures reinforces the focus on a transfer of country rather than a transfer from birth parents to adoptive parents.

The children varied in their capacity to talk about adoption. For many, adoption and the intercountry aspects were private issues. They often distinguished between talking at home and in public settings. It was not always clear whether this was something they had been taught or was because they found it more comfortable than being totally open. One source of reluctance may have been linked to bullying. However, less than half of the eight-to 12-year-olds said they discussed being adopted within their families. Most children in that age range said they would like to visit their country of origin.

The results of the Brodzinsky Openness Questionnaire showed that about half of the teenagers willing to be interviewed experienced some difficulty in communicating with their parents about adoption. Young adults also saw it as a private subject and one they only raised occasionally with a few trusted friends. They were concerned about other people's lack of knowledge and understanding of adoption. Although some of the younger children had obvious curiosity about their history, it was the teenagers and young adults who started to wonder about "what might have been".

A minority of children reported incidents of bullying but many saw them as not serious. Some reported receiving attention they saw as positive because of their skin tone. But others had clearly been upset by bullying which most often was about racial difference. The majority of young adults looking back reported some form of prejudice relating to their adoptive status, skin colour or country of birth.

Major issues for the adoptive parents of these children were a lack of professional knowledge about the specific types of problems which have been found to be consequences of early institutional care, and professionals trying to squeeze children's symptoms into boxes in which they did not fit.

From *A Study of Intercountry Adoption Outcomes in Ireland* (Greene *et al* 2007), commissioned by The Adoption Board from the Children's Research Centre at Trinity College, Dublin

---

Sadly, we do not live in a society that is free from discrimination and prejudice. From subtle connotations in language through to blatant racist abuse, this will not go away. As far back as 1992, Nick Banks in an article in *Adoption & Fostering* concluded, 'to deny the importance of cultural diversity, skin colour and its significance for the black child is to deny the black child confirmation of his or her likely experience...It may be possible for carers and adoption and fostering workers to convince their children or clients that they do not judge or react to people on the basis of their ethnicity or skin colour, but it should be acknowledged that many people in society do...The active, sensitive preparation of black children for racist reality, not an as yet unrealised multi-cultural ideal, is a must!' A decade and more later, this still holds true.

The use of the term "black" to cover people from a wide range of cultural backgrounds continues to generate debate. Here, when it is used in a general way, it is taken to cover any child who has at least one parent who is not part of the majority white population. In talking about themselves and their heritage, for example, Chinese or South Asian people may not describe themselves as "black". They will, however, recognise the relevance of identifying with the social and political issues this terminology denotes. From your child's point of view, the impact of other people's attitudes on them; positive or negative racial identity, and their self worth in relation to others, is a reality whether they are black African, Chinese, Albanian, Guatemalan or of mixed heritage.

A significant percentage of children now placed for adoption have at least one parent who is black African or Caribbean. A look at information about children waiting for families in publications like *Be My Parent* will illustrate this. Some will have spent time in white, temporary foster homes and may not be comfortable initially when placed with black adopters. Many adopters find their starting point is to listen to their child to find out how they view themselves and what messages they have picked up from birth parents or temporary carers about their ethnicity. Children of mixed heritage may have heard negative comments from white birth relatives.

---

## DIRECT IDENTITY WORK AND TACKLING RACISM

**Some extracts from 'Techniques for direct identity work with black children', Nick Banks, *Adoption & Fostering*, 16.3, 1992**

'Imaginative stories can be invented which attempt a (subliminal) reversal of negative connotations of blackness.'

'Basil was a beautiful shiny black beetle. All the other animals wanted to look like him. "We love your glossy black coat," said the white pelican. "I wish I had one as nice as you."'

'Blackness as a positive expressional goal to be achieved can also be useful with statements such as "When you understand more about the world, you will like being black…" However, it needs to be noted that the goal is often not to facilitate the child saying he or she is black, but that of saying he or she does not wish to be white.'

### SOME TECHNIQUES TO CHALLENGE RACISM

**Adapted from material from Scottish Human Services Trust, developed by Priscilla Marongwe from training material on diversity and equal opportunities**

Reflection of feelings.
*You appear to be reacting quite strongly to this.*

Questioning motivation.
*Why would you say that?*

Request reflection.
*Can I ask you to stop and think about what you are saying?*

Questioning information basics.
*Is this fact or opinion? How can you be so certain?*

Assistance request.
*I'd like you to explain that further.*

Reflect personal response.
*I accept that is how you think, but I find it unacceptable, I can't see your point.*

Re-contextualisation.
*If those same things were being said about you, how would you feel?*

---

White adopters of black children sometimes seek help because their child says they want to be white. Nick Banks, in the article referred to above, has various practical suggestions about what he calls 'cognitive ebonisation' which aim to provide children with some sophistication about racism without disabling them with paranoia. This also recognises the care needed not to impose terms like "black" on a child who is rejecting this or avoiding aggravating a child's avoidance of issues. This is a strong argument for starting off on the right foot for positive recognition of difference, open acknowledgement and discussion of derogatory labels and, when reaching adolescence, a willingness to engage in the political debate.

There are now more books and other material available celebrating the achievements of black people. Some black and minority ethnic groups are better represented than others. Building links with people from your child's particular ethnic background should guide you to helpful material. The Letterbox Library, which specialises in multi-cultural books, is another good source (see Useful Books), as well as websites. In finding a language to use with your child, it is also useful to learn culturally specific words, for example, "ghuta" for a Sikh boy's hairstyle.

You will also need a language to use with other people that can model responses for your child. Many white adopters with a black or minority ethnic child report that other people can think that this gives them permission to ask questions or make remarks, which they see as interested or well meaning. When your child is young, there may be comments in front of him or her along the lines of, 'Isn't it wonderful to have done that?'. Your child will need to hear you say that they have brought as much into *your* life. You may then be able to help your child think of a reply like, 'Well, my mum and dad say they think they're lucky to have me too so I think we all like being part of our family'. Questions like, 'So where are you from?' can carry different meanings depending on whether it is asked of a black child in this country or a child who came here from another country. A simple 'I was born in…' may be a polite way of dealing with interest or sometimes it is enough to say, 'Why do you ask?' These are, of course, polite ways of dealing with "friendly" questions. You may prefer to be more direct in indicating that you see such questions as intrusive and none of the enquirer's business.

You will also need to think about how you deal with racist or discriminatory comments, particularly in your child's hearing. Again, black people will have had plenty of time to practise this. Comments may come out differently if made to you as a white person rather than a black person. This makes it all the more important that your child knows you will challenge stereotypes or racist comments.

---

In Chapter 3, reference was make to a book by Renée Wolfs and the guidance from the Netherlands on talking to adopted children at different ages and stages – mainly those adopted intercountry. This used the Brodzinsky ages and stages. Brodzinsky also talked about 'adaptive grieving' – the normal, natural period that mid-primary school-age children may go through as they begin to pick up the losses in adoption and become unsettled for a period while they explore the feelings involved in this. In her book, Renée Wolfs lists what adopted children can grieve for at various ages:

- their birth parents
- their foster parents or the caretakers at the orphanage
- their family tree – the child is no longer linked to the generations
- their place in the original cultural community
- their native country
- the culture of the birth country (smells, food, climate, religion, etc)
- genetic and racial similarities; they look different to their adoptive parents and their friends
- their native language
- any siblings who stayed behind or were adopted by other families
- friends, special possessions, the house, the environment
- the children who stayed at the orphanage
- their original name
- their identity
- their faith and confidence that parents are strong and reliable and that they will always take care of their children, no matter what happens
- their faith that most things in life are honest and just
- their self-esteem
- their autonomy with regard to the right of determining one's own fate/destiny
- their innocence – the accumulation of several losses one has experienced may test the feelings of trust in general
- their bodily integrity, if he or she was abused or raped

This is obviously a huge list and you are not expected to be hit by them all or a number at the same time! They do alert parents, however, to the ranges of concerns that can emerge for their children. Some could relate to all adopted children, others are particularly relevant to children placed transracially or to intercountry adoptions. Renée Wolfs does follow the chapter on adoption-related grief by one looking at ways of dealing with it. Much of the approach links with what is contained in this book on talking about adoption.

## Getting more help

The storybook *Jordan and the Different Day*, by Michaela Morgan (published by the NSPCC/Egmont Books, 2000), may be helpful for young children. The story, following Jordan, a black boy, who is excluded from playing a game because he is different to the other children, looks at respecting differences between people.

Also useful is the CD-ROM *This is Where I Live*, based on young people's views of multi-ethnic Britain. This teaching resource, aimed at 11- to 18-year-olds, is designed to stimulate discussion and provide ideas for activities to help young people express their views about their heritage, sense of belonging, identity and experience of racism. Available from The Runnymede Trust, 7 Plough Yard, London EC2A 3LP, Tel: 020 7377 9222, www.runnymedetrust.org.

There are now an increasing number of resources for children which help to build self-esteem and deal with issues of diversity. One possible source is the Incentive Plus catalogue, which is regularly updated. Many of the resources are geared towards schools – which may also be very positive – but a number of the posters, games and books can be used in normal play and activities with children at home (see www.incentiveplus.co.uk).

Some adoption support services have particular experience in supporting families who have adopted black children or those from minority ethnic backgrounds. The Post Adoption Centre in London is one of these. If you do not live in their area you may not be able to access direct services, but the centre may be able to suggest further material and resources for yourselves as a family or for a worker who is supporting you locally. Post-adoption centres in other parts of the UK may also be able to help.

There are a growing number of websites offering support to parents, some of which have particular relevence to groups where "difference" is an issue. These may range from issues related to the children such as those around special educational needs to those for minority groups of parents such as one for lesbian mothers. This book does not aim to provide either an up-to-date list of these as they will change and develop or any assessment of their value to adoptive parents. What may be helpful is to link with the Adoption UK online community where  you can communicate with other adoptive parents, some of whom may already have experience of trying out such resources.

For intercountry adopters, visit the Intercountry Adoption Centre website (www.icacentre.org.uk) which has information about themed workshops and a range of publications on topics such as returning to the birth country, adoption bereavement, racism and "your story" as well as the publication on schools already referred to. There are also support groups specifically for intercountry adopters. They may focus on children from a particular country, depending on when you adopted. For example, when a number of people adopted from Romania, there were opportunities for these families to get together. With the growth of adoptions from China, there is now a group called Children Adopted from China (www.cach.org.uk). The more general intercountry websites may be able to guide you, or contact OASIS (www.adoptionoverseas.org), another self-help group which many intercountry adopters will know from their first search for information on how to adopt from abroad.

---

## THOUGHTS ON TRANSRACIAL ADOPTION

My parents (who are both white) had nine children, of which four were adopted. I was adopted in 1968, the second mixed-race baby in the family...We were all instilled with the same level of middle-class confidence and were all encouraged to reach the same goals; the prospects of racial hindrance simply didn't come into it. That was their only way of loving me/us: idyllic and colour blind.

However benign their intentions, though, this wasn't representative of society's view of me. Both the black and white community would see my colour first and I'd be instantly judged – be it positively, negatively or with indifference.

I was 19 before I really experienced my first dose of overt racism…I suddenly became aware of the implications of being black, having been blissfully ignorant all my life. I felt ill-equipped to deal with this sudden awareness and subsequent paranoia. I started to feel quite removed from my family…They could never have that intrinsic understanding of racism. Their vicarious empathy felt redundant…

Throughout this necessary and turbulent period it was the indomitable and consistently deep love of my parents and family that encouraged me to work through it. That's what gave me my sense of self and the subsequent strength and confidence to cope. Love gives you the impetus to find your own identity, regardless of colour…being mixed-race can, in theory, allow you access to all cultural areas…But, on the other hand, you don't feel totally accepted by either the white or the black community.

From 'The colour of love', by Clare Gorham, a transracially adopted person, in *In Search of Belonging*, (Harris (ed), 2005)

## Thoughts and feelings

*One area of potential difficulty with a severely disabled child like David is finding ways to help him build a positive self-image. As he struggles against frustration and a growing awareness of his difficulties and limitations, emphasis needs to be placed on those aspects of his life that he can develop and control, for example, personal relationships, intellectual skills, social contact. An adopted or fostered child may also have to cope with the knowledge that he has already been rejected because of his disabilities and David often seeks reassurance that I knew he couldn't walk and still wanted him. It is painful to answer his many questions about why he can't walk or write or draw, but I have always answered truthfully but simply, and it does seem to help him to verbalise his feelings about his disabilities.*

*Possibly the most vital thing of all is to try and stay in touch with our children, to talk with them, to learn from them. If you are white, you may not face the frequent put-downs and slights, or worse, that they do, but you can share their humiliations and embarrassments, and discuss with them ways of dealing with racism – when to confront people or when to walk away with dignity. You can play your part too by refusing to watch unacceptable programmes on TV, and by openly expressing your disgust over racist comments and action expressed in the media or by people you meet. These skills can be made easier if you can ask black people to help you.*

*Every day, your child hears the word "black" used to mean "wrong" and the word "white" to mean*

*"right". Think of "getting a black mark",
"blacklisted", "in a black mood", "blackmail",
"black market" and so on. All these terms have a
negative meaning. Where does this leave your
black child? No wonder the phrase "black is
beautiful" was coined: black people need to
believe in themselves, just like everyone else does.
At least in your family and social circle, you can try
to avoid using words in this way. Try to put yourself
in your child's place, and be sensitive to their
feelings. If you go on using "black" to mean
something bad, you too are helping to give your
child a poor impression of their colour and
themselves.*

# If you are a step-parent or other relative

*We thought adopting the children would make us into a "real" family and Colin would be much more their father than before. But actually it caused some problems. The kids didn't want him to order them about, and he felt that with the added responsibility, he could. It took ages before they accepted him and even now there are some arguments about it.*

If you are a step-parent who has adopted, or who is thinking of adopting, your step-children, much of what appears elsewhere in this book will also be relevant to you and your step-children. Step-families are on the increase, but adoption by step-parents has decreased. Because currently adoption cuts off legal ties with one birth parent, other arrangements are now often seen as more appropriate, particularly where the child has strong links with the absent parent (referred to as the "other birth parent" in this section).

There are other legal ways for step-parents to secure their relationship with a child in their family. Until recently, however, at least half of the adoptions in the UK were step-parent adoptions, and there are still a sizable number. If you adopted before the implementation of the Children (Scotland) Act 1995 or the Adoption and Children Act 2002, your children will have an adoption certificate naming both parents as adoptive parents. People usually find it very odd initially that the birth parent in step-parent adoptions legally became the child's adoptive parent! Your child is also likely to find this very strange. They will need to understand their personal story well before encountering such legal anomalies. If you are just thinking about adopting now in England, Wales or Scotland, it will make more sense to you – and ultimately your child – that it is now only the step-parent who will acquire parental responsibilities and rights through adoption while the birth parent remains the same. Northern Ireland has not yet changed this situation but it is under discussion, along with all the other potential changes in adoption there.

In thinking ahead to talking about this, it might be helpful to keep a copy of the original birth certificate safely. Whether or not the birth father is named on this, his position will be part of your child's history.

## Adopting pre-school step-children

A situation that often arises is when a single mother subsequently marries a man who is not the father of their child and they wish to confirm the new family unit, particularly where the step-father is the only "father" the child has known. The legal process of adoption is often already started when the question of telling the child is brought up, and for people who have not been prepared for that, it is a good time to begin. You may find some of the ideas suggested earlier for adopters of non-related children can be adapted for your situation.

## IF YOU'RE THINKING ABOUT ADOPTION

BAAF has produced two leaflets about step-parents and adoption, one for England and Wales, and one for Scotland. These spell out the advantages and disadvantages of adopting for step-parents and tell you where to get more information. They are available from BAAF (see Useful Books).

There are not the same commercially produced simple story books for children in this situation, but BAAF has produced an illustrated book for children called *Jo's Story* that tells the story of a girl adopted by her step-father (see Useful Books). Many families have also found it helpful to make their own story books with photographs. It is useful to sort out at this stage any areas that might be awkward to discuss as these may be different from other adoptions. For example, the child's parent (usually the mother) may still have very personal feelings about the absent birth parent – she may be angry, feel let down or embarrassed at the thought of talking about a relationship that she may regret or have pushed into the past. However, at this early stage, one or two simple facts, like the father's name and perhaps a couple of child-friendly details, are all that are needed to help establish the truth and get over the initial hurdle in a gentle way. Fuller explanations can come later and you have time to sort out wording with which you are comfortable. Sometimes the step-parent fears that somehow he is in a secondary position as parent to this child and thought can be given to positive wording which emphasises that in marrying the birth mother he chose not only his partner but also freely embraced her child and made a commitment to both. This can be particularly useful as a focus if the "telling" has been left to a later stage when the step-parent may have concerns about the knowledge undermining a valued and well-established relationship with the child.

## Adopting older children

For older children, other problems may appear. In cases of divorce, for example, the child may deeply resent the legal loss of the other birth parent. After all, divorce was not the child's idea and neither was the step-parent. The special relationship a child often has with a single parent may be seen as put at risk by a step-parent. And children may worry that if they start to love their new step-parent, they'll somehow risk losing their other birth parent's love. This sort of adjustment to new and changing relationships can be tricky in any family, and is likely to have been around and dealt with before adoption came onto the agenda. Parentline Plus (incorporating the former National Stepfamily Association) can provide both information and support (see Useful Organisations).

---

**WHAT IS A PARENT?**

To help a child understand, it might be useful to explain something about what being a parent means.

First and foremost, it means giving you life (your genetic inheritance) and includes:

- the way you look;
- the way your brain and body work;
- some of the things you are good at and like to do;
- some of the things you find difficult and don't like.

Secondly, it means caring for you and bringing you up:

● loving you and minding what happens to you;
● encouraging you and comforting you;
● looking after you physically;
● teaching you all the things you need to know until you're independent.

Thirdly, it means taking responsibility for you:

● making important decisions about things like schooling and future plans;
● providing for you in material ways;
● representing your needs until you're old enough to do this yourself.

A child needs all these things, and for most children, they all come from the birth parents. But for adopted children, including those adopted by step-parents, where the birth parent(s) aren't in a position to take on the second and third areas of responsibility, it means having two sets of parents.

---

These issues, which arise in many step-families, can come to the fore again in considering adoption. Adoption may make the child seem more secure, or it may increase feelings of loss about the other birth parent. Whatever the situation, the child needs to be consulted and listened to. If they are 12 or over in Scotland they will be asked to sign their agreement to their adoption. Other children need to be aware that their wishes will be taken into account. Sometimes adults reach decisions that do not completely accord with the child's wishes and children will need to be helped to understand the reasons for this. It hurts when it feels like you're losing a parent and equally it can be confusing to some to think they have three parents. Of course, not all children adopted by their step-fathers ever knew their birth fathers. But where the birth father is known, especially if he still keeps in contact with the child, it's up to you to make things clear. Life story books, as described earlier in Chapter 5, can work wonders here, with family trees showing where everyone fits in. The time originally spent talking about the separation when it happened, the consideration about which parent the child would live with, contact with the other parent and then the introduction of new partners is vital. This forms the foundation, not only for considering any further changes such as adoption, but also for the establishment of open communication. It's hard work, but so are most relationships that are worth having.

Talking about the possibility of adoption may also bring up other changes which may have happened, such as the birth of other children. The implications of these changes will vary. You may be very aware of the reactions of your child if, after gaining a step parent following a divorce, their birth parent and step-parent subsequently have a child together. Thinking of adopting may be part of assuring a child of their place in the family and their full acceptance by the step-parent. Feelings may be very different if the thought of adoption links in a child's mind with anxieties about weakening a valued relationship with their other birth parent who may also have a new partner and other children. Even if it is awkward, you may need to think about talking to an ex-partner so that any fears your child may have are recognised and addressed.

## Other adoptive situations

Some children are adopted by members of their extended family, like grandparents or aunts. In the past this was often in order to hide an illegitimate pregnancy and was shrouded in secrecy. For adopted adults this has led to special complications, not only about the shock of discovering their adoption but also because family secrets can create all sorts of tensions. They may struggle with how much different family members know or what thoughts and memories they might have of earlier events. Over the years this situation has changed, and normally families are much more open in responding to the difficulties of individual members, looking for other solutions to secure children within the extended family. Sometimes, however, such adoptions happen in the hope of providing security for a particular child. There is, for example, a clear difference between children knowing that they were adopted by their grandparents, and grandparents adopting a grandchild but bringing this child up as though they are the child's parents, which obviously complicates all other family relationships.

It is easy enough to say the same principles apply to any adoption, namely, that children need to know and understand their origins, and that this is based on a gradually growing awareness linked to children's ability to understand at different stages of development. For such in-family adoptions there are some additional distinctive features. Firstly, it is not so much about the child integrating the knowledge of two families – the birth and the adoptive family – but rather about feeling confident of his or her position within the whole extended family. This, however, may still only be the extended family of one parent, and the absent birth parent may be more firmly excluded, while still being part of the child's origins. Secondly, when grandparents talk with the child about his or her birth parents, they are also discussing their own son or daughter and this can be upsetting, particularly if that son or daughter has been involved in a very problematic lifestyle like alcohol or drug misuse. If you are in this position you may need to call upon the support of other trusted family members or one of the adoption counselling services. Similar issues arise from talking with children about their origins and intimate family matters in many circumstances. The growing range of adoption support and advice services are for *everyone* with experience of adoption – not just if it was formally arranged by an adoption agency.

Reproduction assisted by new techniques of fertility treatment may now be another topic which is difficult to broach with children and which needs careful planning. As an example of "finding the right words", a book called *My Story*, available from the Donor Conception Network, which is aimed at children about four or five years old, gives a simple explanation of donor insemination (see Useful Books). A new contribution to the debate about the similarities and differences in adoption or assisted reproduction is *Who am I? Experiences of donor conception*, (Alexina McWhinnie (ed), 2006), published by IDREOS Education Trust. One particular response to infertility that directly leads to adoption is that of surrogacy. As in step-parent adoption, this can have different implications for two parents as the child may be genetically linked to the father but not the mother, although adopted by both. As surrogate mothers usually have other children, there is also the question of talking about their biological half-siblings as well as finding the right words to talk about why their birth mother would agree to have a baby whom she would give away.

Not only are these services developing all the time, but there is also more consideration given now to letting children know about their origins. As your child grows up, it is worth keeping in touch with these services or self-help groups, such as the Infertility Network UK, as new ideas and material are constantly being developed.

---

**Thoughts and feelings**

*Explaining it all to the children was the difficult bit…that they'd still be loved by their father and they should still love him, and he'd still be their father. The fact that I'd be married to someone else didn't mean that they couldn't still see him. Then there were all the questions about what to call my second husband – and who to make cards for on Father's Day. We got round that one by getting them to make two each, and I think they ended up being quite proud of the fact – it put them one up on the others in their class.*

---

*I was nine when my parents divorced and Mum remarried when I was 11. At first I got on really well with my step-father and wanted him to adopt me, because we lost touch with my real father really quickly. But when I was a teenager it was nothing but rows over everything I did. Then I wished he hadn't adopted me! But we're OK now.*

---

*We decided to adopt Rachel when she was seven. She knew we were her grandparents and who her mum was – but she wanted to be the same as everyone else at school. She called us 'Mum and Dad' and she wanted to see us treated like that by people like her teachers. Fortunately our daughter agreed it was best too.*

---

# Talking about yourself

*Having married in the spring of 1997, we had assumed that an imminent pregnancy would follow, just as it had for so many of our friends before us. It was not to be. The path to accepting that we would never have a birth child was long and hard. Eventually we managed to work our way through it. We came to realise that we could still be loving parents to a child who needed us. We could adopt and offer a child a home where they could feel safe and secure and loved.*
From *'Commitment and a dose of patience'*, by Maria James, in *Be My Parent News & Features*, September 2007

Much of this book has been about children's need to know about their origins and find answers to the big question, 'Why was I adopted?' Adoptive parents spend a lot of time thinking about the best ways to help their child understand their background.

Young children naturally start from being the centre of their own world, therefore first questions will centre around themselves. As they grow older, they develop their ability to recognise other people's views and feelings. Comment has already been made about the thoughtful, caring side shown by many adopted people as they have grown up learning about the pressures on their birth parents. Equally, many adopted people when they get together, also express their respect for the feelings of their adoptive parents. The other questions that come up for children may well be 'Why did you decide to adopt?' and 'Why me?'

As adults, we are often unaccustomed to talking about ourselves with our children. You will need to consider the right balance of what is helpful for your child to know and what is private. Birth parents have also pointed out their sense of embarrassment at the amount that their children might be told about them. We are not talking here about sharing all sorts of intimate details. We have, however, already referred to the use of words like "real parents". For adopted children their adoptive parents are the most "real" ones in their day-to-day lives, so understanding their perspective and what made them the people they are, is very important.

The novelist and poet Jackie Kay, who was herself adopted, wrote *The Adoption Papers* (published by Bloodaxe Books, 1991), reflecting the voices of the birth parent, adoptive parent and child. In 'The Telling Part', she looks at the idea of the 'real mother' and the impact on a child of questioning this.

'After mammy telt me she wisnae my real mammy, I was scared to death she was gonna melt or something, or mibbe disappear in the dead of night and somebody would say she is a fairy godmother.'

In a later interview, Jackie Kay said about adoption:

'It's to do with how much biology is imposed on you and how much of what you have as an individual comes from your environment. In the book I'm saying that "the real mother is the adoptive mother – the one who brought me up."' (*Everywoman*, March 1992)

This is not about easy assurances, and *The Adoption Papers* reflects painful feelings from all viewpoints.

Much is written in adoption about losses and the reality for adoptive parents that at times the child will trigger reminders of their own former losses. This is also an area where there are opportunities to help children think about coping with those losses and moving on.

This is particularly relevant if you come to adoption because of infertility, which is the reality in the majority of adoptions. It may help your child both to know that, like him or her, you understand that things do not always work out as you might have planned or hoped, and also that if you face up to that, other ways forward can be found. Good things can follow and positive alternatives chosen. Many adopters have expressed their initial surprise when attending adoption preparation groups about just how much is involved. Some of this is about recognising that adoption is a different way to build a family. Unlike the earlier focus of the medical investigations and treatment aimed at fertility difficulties, adoption can never claim to heal infertility. It is important, if your child shows interest in knowing why you adopted, that you consider the implications of what you say. Could your child feel responsible for making you feel better after such a hard time? Could they be anxious to be as good as the child you might have given birth to? What might they feel if you later had a birth child? Neither you nor your child are likely to need to go into the reasons for your infertility or all that you went through at that time. What is more important is to give some flavour of the thinking you went through in planning to adopt – your recognition that even though one door had closed, a new opportunity had opened up.

Some time ago, BAAF produced a booklet by Kulwinder Sparks (see Useful Books), a teenager who was adopted. It included responses from some families to whom she had sent a questionnaire and also questions to the adopters like, 'What made you decide that you wanted to adopt?', 'What did you feel during the waiting period?', 'What was the image you had of the child you first thought of when you had the idea that you wanted to adopt?' and 'What was the image that you had of the child after you had your home studies?' One of the conclusions as an adopted person she shared with others was:

'So you can see that your parents go through quite a stressful time. They have a lot of waiting and worrying to do about the present and the future as well as having their past raked up and having to come to terms with things again that may have happened to them, which all get brought up during the home studies.' (*Why Adoption*, BAAF and Thomas Coram Foundation, 1995.)

While you as adoptive parents are being prepared and assessed for what lies ahead, so preparation is happening with older children who cannot return home. Part of this is thinking about different sorts of families. Just as you find out about them, they will want details about you. You may well have prepared a book, photograph album or video for your child. This is the start of filling in the gaps, not just the gaps in your knowledge of your child, but also the child's knowledge of this family that she or he is going to join.

Like the information listed in Chapter 3, this starts with concrete information. The children interviewed in *Adopted Children Speaking* had very vivid memories of learning about their new family and meeting them. A more reflective view was expressed by one girl who said, 'You both have to make the effort to know each other and to feel comfortable about living with each other'.

Like any other relationship, this emphasises its reciprocal nature. While you may be learning what makes your child "tick", she or he will be weighing you up too!

The question of choice also comes up here. Most parents and children do not choose each other! Adoption implies a choice but often this is not an even one and has lots of restrictions. Some elements of this can be positive for your child but the idea needs to be used realistically. You may have chosen to go down the route of adoption but the reasons for that may have been varied. The reasons for a step-parent or relative adoption are based in family relationships that are very different from deciding to adopt a non-related child through an adoption agency. You may have spent a long time deciding whether you should go down the intercountry route or, if you adopt in the UK, what age range you could consider, or whether you could adopt a sibling group. At the time you were doing all this, it was usually theoretical. Now in bringing up your child, these choices will have become personal.

Many older children can be reassured by knowing that their adoptive parents knew a lot about them, "warts and all", and chose to go ahead with a "match". Recollections and reminders of what drew you to a particular child can be very important, along with confident statements about 'We knew what you needed and we felt, yes, we can do that'.

Choice does not operate the same way for children. Babies and small children rely on choices made on their behalf, perhaps first by their birth parents who sought an adoptive placement, and then later, by the agency responsible making the best plans for their care. As your child grows older, he or she may want to know more about the reasons for this.

In other chapters, we have referred to some of the dilemmas that can come up sometimes, for example, if a family cannot be found that reflects a child's culture, ethnicity or religion, or if a foster carer can only offer to adopt one child out of a sibling group. A "later life letter" from the social worker at the time may be helpful in confirming the reasons for the choice.

Older children may appear to be involved in the choice but in reality, this means that they should have been told as much as they could understand about the plan for adoption and their views taken into account. Despite everyone's best efforts, a move is still going to be strange and unsettling, and not feel like a conscious choice. As one child said, 'You have to get used to the home, have to get used to where you live and the places outside. It's not what you are used to, new next door neighbours. You have to get used to everything really.'

Tuning into your child's confused feelings at this time and allowing
him or her space to express doubts and confusion, even if you are
desperate for him or her to settle in, will create a climate of respect.
From the outset, your child will be picking up how much you are
giving of yourselves, as well as responding to their needs.

At the peak of adoption placement of babies by relinquishing
mothers, the stigma of being a single parent was too great for many
to contemplate. Adoptive parents were, by definition, married
couples. Now, in a social climate where many types of family
structures exist, single parents, same-sex partners, step-families, as
well as traditional nuclear families, are all accepted as adoptive
parents. Children too need to learn that adoption is not always
about a "new mummy and daddy". Adopters in less traditional
households are already likely to be familiar with these debates and
to have discussed this thoroughly before adopting. This will give you
a good foundation for answering questions from your child.
Feedback from your agency both about why they thought you
would be good adopters and also why you were linked with your
particular child may provide you with more ideas.

Alongside thinking of what you will say to your child to explain your
circumstances in a "non-traditional" household, you will need to
think about equipping them to answer questions from friends and
people outside the family. Children may need help to understand
having three mums or dads – two they live with and a former birth
one! They may need a confident riposte to avoid a potential bullying
attempt, such as maybe that you can't have too much of a good
thing! They will also need to be able to have a more informed and
informative conversation with friends who are interested and open
to thinking about diversity. You may need to have strategies to
handle times when the school curriculum creates added problems
for children in non-traditional households. Some schools are
sensitive to this but it can still come up. Of course there are likely to
be other children in the class living with single parents, same-sex
parents, step-parents or grandparents. What is different for your
child is the conscious choice to place them with you for adoption. If
your child was older when they came to you this may come up quite

early, so you need to be prepared. There are now a wider range of children's resources to draw on – particularly children's books reflecting more diverse households. BAAF's books *Picnic in the Park*, and *Josh and Jaz have Three Mums* may be helpful for younger children (see Useful Books).

Sometimes when children are older, they like to see some of their adoption documents. Until the recent changes in legislation in England, Wales and Scotland which enabled unmarried and same-sex couples to adopt jointly, they could come across the anomaly that their experience of growing up in a two-parent household was not reflected in the official documents. They will need to be aware of this and the reasons for it from you. Older children may be aware of the attention this aspect of "who can adopt" caused in the media and the different views expressed at the time. This may recur if and when similar adoption changes in Northern Ireland are debated. Some may be happy to add their comments! Depending on where you live in the UK, you may need to clarify what was – or was not – possible at the time you adopted.

---

### Thoughts and feelings

*In our family when one of the children has said, 'I wish I grew in your tummy, Mum,' I have said, 'Well, I would have liked to grow babies in my tummy but if I had it wouldn't have been you and you would have been given to a different mummy and daddy, so I think it's better as it is.'*

*The whole process is there to make you
understand yourself – to make you really ask,
'what am I doing?' and 'why am I doing this?'*

*If I was choosing an adoptive parent, I would
choose my mum. Apart from that, I would choose
someone who didn't smack and shout – unless she
shouted for fun.*

---

*I think single people should be able to adopt and I
think nearly everyone should be able to adopt,
apart from people who are a bit mean and hit their
children.*

---

# 12

# How adopted children feel

*Whenever my parents told me off or wanted me to do something I didn't want to do, I'd say 'My real mum would have let me' or 'She'd have understood'. I didn't mean it ... I'd no idea whether she would or not, but it was a way of getting back at them. Somehow they put up with me even when I was trying to be so awkward like this. I even ran away twice but I went back. Later, when I met my first mother, I felt I had much more in common with them than with her after all. I didn't realise till years later how much this must have hurt them.*

Of course, every child's experience of adoption is personal and unique. Below are just a few brief examples of children's and young people's perceptions of their adoption. There are a number of books and specialist magazines that include further experiences of being adopted (see Useful Books).

When I first came to this family I was very frightened because I had been moved from different homes before – they had been horrid. So I thought that because the other homes were not very nice to me that this family was going to be horrid. The first night I came I was not used to so many people around the house and I was very confused, but soon – after about four weeks – I got used to my surroundings. Sometimes when social workers came I ran away into my bedroom because I thought that each time I would be taken away. I used to always think about the past. But my foster parents taught me to look into the future and what I would do and not what I had done.

---

I like living with my mummy and daddy and little sister. I grew in Maureen's tummy. I went to hospital to be born but then I had to live with somebody else. I was very sad but I loved my new parents. They loved me. I was adopted by my mummy and daddy. We went to court to see if I could live with them. The judge said yes. I grew up to be a big girl and now I am six. I wanted a little sister so Mummy and Daddy said I could. Once again we went to court to see if my little sister could live with us. The judge said yes. My sister is two now and I like playing with her.

---

I can think back to situations when, as a child, people were trying to protect me from some harsh realities that I had to face eventually as an adult anyway. If these people had been less protective and willing to talk, I think that I might have been better able to deal with some of the stressful situations I had to face as a young adult. When I had problems with people, and I honestly knew that those problems arose because I was black, people looking after me would say, 'Just ignore them, they are only ignorant and don't know you,' rather than helping me to cope by talking such issues through with me in order to help me understand better.

The fact that I was not born to my parents has never ever worried or saddened me; with loving and caring parents as I am lucky enough to have, whether or not we are related by blood does not matter to any of us. I feel that my sister and I belong as much to our parents as any of my friends do to their natural parents. My reaction, when asked what I feel about my other family in another country, is that I don't have another family; I've only ever known one mother, one father and one sister. We are all able to talk very freely about my sister's and my first families but they seem so distant, hardly connected with us at all. It seems slightly unreal to me. Maybe I should feel closer to my first parents. I don't know. After all, it was thanks to them that I am part of a very close family now. I hope they don't miss me; I hope they are able to speak about me as I am able to speak about them. Although I was born to them and I knew them for nine months, I feel it's not so much who you're born to, it's who you spend your life with that matters.

---

I wanted to be adopted when I understood what it meant. I did so want to be part of a family and stay for good. I began to get very ill because I wanted to be adopted. When I was adopted I cried with happiness. Now I have been adopted I feel safe. I can stay with my family for as long as I please and that will be for as long as I live. I love my family very much.

# 13

# How birth parents feel

*I'm a mother who had a child nearly forty years ago, alone. The baby's father was not married and he could have married me if he had wanted to. I loved the father and I loved the baby all through the pregnancy and I loved her enough to give her away so that she could have a family. I would not have considered adoption if I had not thought that the adoptive parents had a lot more to offer than I could. My cherished wish is to meet them and to know how she is getting on.*

As has been pointed out already in this book, it's important to try and understand your child's birth parents so that you can help him or her with knowledge about them. It's often difficult not to judge people, but you may not know all the circumstances. As you can imagine, mothers and fathers who give up their children do not, by and large, do it easily. There is usually a lot of heartache and emotional turmoil involved. If your child came to you as a baby, you may like to read about some of the experiences of vulnerable young mothers (see *Half a Million Women* and *Within me, Without me* in Useful Books). If your child was older, as is now increasingly the case, think of the circumstances and try to put yourself in the birth parents' place. Remember that they will certainly feel a deep sense of regret and guilt at having "lost" their child. Almost always, if they eventually agreed to the adoption it was because they believed that it was the best for their child and was the most responsible thing they could do in the circumstances.

If the birth parents of your child did not agree to the adoption, they may be left with a whole mixture of confused feelings. Mixed in with anger or guilt, there may be a tremendous sense of loss of a child of whom they have strong memories, especially if they had lived together for a considerable period (see *Still Screaming* in Useful Books). Yet often these birth parents not only have extra problems in many areas of their lives, but have also cut themselves off from either family or professional support or find it hard to use or accept this.

As the years go by, if there is no contact between the birth parents and the adopted child, many birth parents feel an overwhelming sense of loss, particularly around the date of the child's birth. As the time of the child's sixteenth or eighteenth birthday approaches, many anticipate the telephone call or letter that means their child wants to make contact. For some, this may be based on a hope stemming from their memory of what they were told many years ago, while others may have picked up more recent information from the media. If nothing happens, they are kept in a state of uncertainty which is never far from the surface, though it may last years or even a lifetime.

Some birth parents, of course, feel differently. They may be in the position of having married and had other children and may never even have admitted to their partner that there was a previous child. They may feel dread at the thought of the "knock on the door". Just as openness about adoption is the best thing, so openness about one's past is often the only way to real peace of mind in these circumstances.

## WHO CAN AND CAN'T TRACE

As the law stands at present in the UK, adopted children can see their original birth certificates at 16 in Scotland or 18 in England, Wales and Northern Ireland, and this gives them identifying information that can help them to try to trace their birth parents.

More attention is now paid to birth parents' need for information about their child's progress if no contact arrangements were made when their child was placed. The Adoption and Children Act 2002 provides for the setting up of an intermediary service so that an adopted adult can be told that a birth relative has enquired about them. The Act applies only to England and Wales. Intermediary support agencies in these countries can provide these services. Birth parents cannot be given information identifying their child and his or her new name without the agreement of the adopted person. Because this has retrospective implications and adoptive families were not given preparation for it, it is possible for an adopted person over 18 to record a full or partial veto with the agency which holds the adoption records. An intermediary would check if there is any such information from the adopted person recorded either on adoption records or on the Adoption Contact Register. Details can be found on the website www.adoptionsearchreunion.org.uk.

A number of adoption support services throughout the UK had

already been making enquiries on behalf of birth parents before this legal change in England and Wales. This should continue in the other parts of the UK. Any subsequent decisions about sharing information or meeting depend on the willingness of the adopted adult. Again, no identifying information would be shared without consent.

BAAF has produced a leaflet, *Child from the Past*, with information for parents who placed a child for adoption years ago in England and Wales. The charity, Supporting Adults Affected by Adoption – NORCAP, is also a useful source of information (see Useful Organisations).

## Explaining adoption to the birth parent's children

Many parents whose children were adopted in the past go on to have other children. They then have to decide whether or not to tell these children about their earlier child. In this situation, as in the others described in this book, honesty is usually the best policy. Whether or not these children have the right to know that they have another brother or sister is an interesting question. But if the adopted child decides to look for his or her birth family, these siblings and the rest of the family are likely to find out about it anyway. However, parents, particularly mothers, in this position often find it very difficult to tell their children. They may worry that the children would be afraid of being given up too (depending on their age), or how it would make them appear – callous, hard-hearted, perhaps promiscuous. It can be very difficult for young people today, growing up surrounded by single parent families, to understand how different the world once was and what a stigma was attached to "illegitimacy". Nonetheless, the truth is still the best answer, with whatever detail the child can cope with at their age.

For other birth parents now, their family circumstances may be much more complex as were the reasons surrounding their child's adoption. This may include full or half-brothers and sisters still at home with them or in other forms of care. While you may be struggling to find the right words to talk to your adopted child, the birth parents may be struggling even more to talk to other children or members of their extended family, especially while they may be feeling very bad about themselves and how they have coped with their lives.

Adopted children often don't seek out their birth parents as they feel they were given away or not wanted. This is far from the truth. I was 18, naive, and vulnerable. I stayed at the mother and baby home until the birth of my daughter. We had choices but, looking back, I was manipulated into giving up my child: 'Surely, if you love your daughter, you want the best for her – two loving parents who can give her a good and secure home, etc.' So I was made to feel I had to give her up, love my baby as I did! But in all the time before the birth of my child and after, not one person said to me, 'Have you thought of keeping your child?' Now, married with three further children, when each was born (and many more times besides) I have cried for the baby I should have kept. So my message to adopted people is: don't feel you were given up or unwanted. I wasn't the only young girl at the home and the majority were in the same boat.

## Thoughts and feelings

*When I finally decided that the best thing for the kids was not to go on trying to bring them up myself, I felt very guilty at first. People didn't want to know me. But the ups and downs of me going in and out of hospital had really messed their lives up and I wanted them to have some stability. I know now that I was right, and not everybody else. Though I've missed them, they've had a much better chance than they would have had with me, as things turned out. I still think of them a lot, especially at Christmas and birthdays.*

*My thoughts for my daughter's adoptive parents have always been kind. I hope that I will meet them. I know it's a lot to ask, but hopefully as our society is changing, they will not see me as a threat. I can understand their attachment, the pride and love they have shared. The extra love I have cannot hurt. Even if the only mistake I made was having her adopted, I have had to accept so many things concerning her. I hope that they will accept that I exist and that I love her, and that I also love her enough not to try and tear her away from a family that has brought her up and still loves her.*

# Tracing birth parents

*As I got to my teens, I thought I might search one day. When I was 18, I applied for the information that was around my birth, but then I decided not to do anything about the searching immediately after that. I wanted to know more about my birth parents, but I think it was really more about me, more than thinking about the reasons why it never worked out and why I was adopted…the sheet I got was fairly basic information, but at the time it was enough.*

From *Searching Questions* (Feast and Philpot, 2003)

When they reach a certain age, adopted children in the UK have the right to see their original birth certificate. This means that they can find out the name of their birth mother, and sometimes father, if they do not already know it. They can also see the address their mother gave at that time. With this information they can, if they choose, try to trace their birth parent(s) and perhaps make contact with them. Not all adopted children do, and certainly not all at the age of 16 or 18, but the numbers are growing rapidly.

In Scotland it was always possible for adopted people to have access to their original birth certificate from the age of 17 (now 16), and so birth parents and adoptive parents should have been made aware of this at the time the adoption plan was being made. In England and Wales the right of adopted people from the age of 18 to see their original birth certificate was only introduced in 1976, so of course there are many birth parents who gave up their child for adoption before that time expecting never to have any future contact with them. Because of this, children who were adopted before that law came into force have to have an interview with a counsellor (usually a social worker) before they can see their birth certificate. This helps to give them a chance to think about the possible consequences for themselves and their birth parents if they wish to seek more information and actually consider tracing that birth parent. In Northern Ireland, the equivalent change in legislation was later so people adopted there before 1987 need counselling before getting their original birth certificate. Children adopted more recently are not required to see a counsellor before getting their birth records. However, the effects of this step can be far-reaching and very emotional, so talking it over with a counsellor or objective outsider is strongly recommended.

The Children Act 1989 included provision for the Registrar General to set up the Adoption Contact Register for England and Wales. The Register is in two parts – Part I is a list of adopted people who have chosen to register and Part II a similar list of birth parents and other relatives of an adopted person. The Register provides a safe and confidential way for birth parents and other relatives to assure an adopted person that contact would be welcome and to give a current address; a leaflet giving full details is available from them (see below). In Scotland a similar adoption contact register called Birthlink has been available for a number of years based in a voluntary adoption agency (see below) and there is also provision in Northern Ireland.

## Seeking information and making contact

Very many adopted adults now seek further information about their birth parents or go on to make contact. Whether or not they are required to seek counselling, a growing number do seek support through what can be a very emotional period and there is more and more knowledge and experience around now about what can be involved (see *I'm Here Waiting; Adoption, Search and Reunion; Searching Questions* and *The Adoption Triangle Revisited* in Useful Books, and also the website www.adoptionsearchreunion.org.uk).

---

**THE ADOPTION CONTACT REGISTER AND BIRTHLINK**

The purpose of the Adoption Contact Register in England and Wales is to put adopted people and their parents or other relatives in touch with each other where this is what they both want. The Register provides a safe and confidential way for birth parents and other relatives to assure an adopted person that contact would be welcome and to give a current address. A leaflet giving more information can be obtained from:

The Adoption Contact Register, The General Register Office (England and Wales), Room C201, Trafalgar Road, Southport, Merseyside PR8 2HH, Tel. 0151 471 4830. You will be required to complete an application form and there is a fee for registration.

In Northern Ireland, the Adoption Contact Register is held at The General Register Office, Oxford House, 49/55 Chichester

Street, Belfast BT1 4HL Tel. 028 9025 2000. Their website is at www.groni.gov.uk.

Birthlink is Scotland's adoption contact register. It is confidential and it is a central point of contact for all those involved in the adoption process. Based in a voluntary social work charity, Birthlink is a free source of information though there may be a charge for some of the more in-depth services. Further information can be obtained from Birthlink, 21 Castle Street, Edinburgh EH2 3DN, Tel. 0131 225 6441

---

Some do not wish to go further than filling in some gaps in background information; some may seek only limited contact via an intermediary; and others go on to seek direct contact and are involved in reunions. These can initially be highly charged emotionally and may or may not approach anywhere near the hopes or expectations of the individuals concerned. It can be useful to have relatively up-to-date information about birth parents so as to be as realistic as possible about their circumstances. However, some adopted people have an overwhelming need to try and make contact at certain points in their lives and may need a lot of support if it does not work out as they hoped. To find out more about the whole range of experiences of reunions, you could contact Supporting Adults Affected by Adoption – NORCAP (see Useful Organisations) which produces a regular newsletter, and there are some helpful books listed in Useful Books. A book titled *Special and Odd*, by James Mulholland, tells his story of meeting his birth mother many years after having being adopted.

Although they may want to explore these options for themselves, some adopted adults are also very concerned about the impact of that wish on their adoptive parents. Some do not search until after their adoptive parents' death. Others may find it hard to talk with their parents in case they cause pain or distress. On the other hand, some adoptive parents feel sad that they may be left out of their adopted son or daughter's search for their birth parents after being

so intimately involved in their formative years. With greater
openness now, this is another area for sensitivity in sharing.

## How will you feel?

It's important for you to try not to see any interest your child might
have in his or her birth parents as a threat to his or her relationship
with you. Try to put yourself in their place. Wouldn't you be
intrigued to know what your birth mother was like – what she
looked like and how she felt about you? Or to find out a bit more
about your father? It's a natural instinct and much the best way for
you to deal with it is to be as positive as possible.

You know more about your child than anyone and you can help
them. If you say something like, 'When you're 18 you can get your
birth certificate and if you want to trace your birth parents I can
help you,' your son or daughter will be more likely to involve you
and won't feel embarrassed (as many do) or that they are being
unfair to you. You won't run the risk, as many adopters have, of not
being told that their adopted son or daughter is trying to trace their
birth parents. But if, however positive you are, your son or daughter
still feels uneasy and decides to leave you out or to discuss the
search with someone else rather than you, try not to feel hurt. It can
be a very difficult and emotional time for them. Having more than
one set of parents is confusing. This does not mean that they are
rejecting or devaluing all the parenting and love you have given
them over many years (the 'What is a parent?' box in Chapter 10
might help). It also helps to remember that many of the services
established to offer adoption support find that adopted people who
embark on tracing do so in small steps, often with long gaps in
between. Even the most secure adopted adult can be surprised by
the emotional impact of some new small personal link to a birth
parent and need to step back for a while.

It is very important to recognise that adopters, however supportive
they are, can feel irrationally but nonetheless painfully hurt when a
reunion actually occurs. Many have told us this and were not

expecting it. Remember, it's OK to feel this way and it may be useful to talk to another adoptive parent or counsellor. Self-help groups, such as the long established Adoption UK, are there because they understand this (see Useful Organisations).

Many reunion stories reflect adoptions made many years ago of babies relinquished with no thought or provision for later tracing. The situation is very different now for children placed with contact arrangements; those with ongoing links, if not with birth parents, then perhaps with siblings and also for non-relinquished children from potentially dangerous backgrounds. Access to an original birth certificate is not an issue if, by the time your child was placed, she or he knew their original name and birth parents. Of course, if your child has had direct contact throughout childhood, the questions are not about tracing but about handling the different relationships into adult life. Contact arrangements, however, may falter so there can be a gap in knowledge of what has been happening within the birth family. Many adopters now keep in touch with their adoption agency and so have a channel to advice on any further steps if their child wants to find birth family members again. A number of teenagers are now seeking services as part of their search for identity before they have the official right of access to records. In some situations, adoptive parents may be worried if young people are embarking on further steps without knowing or absorbing their full history. In a few cases this includes possible risks to their child springing from the background information. This may be particularly so if the young person is going through a rebellious phase. There are now so many possible scenarios it would be impossible for this book to cover all eventualities. Remember, there are adoption services available throughout the UK because it is now accepted that adoption is a life-long commitment and that adopted people and their adoptive families should be able to ask for help, advice and support at any time.

The aim of this book has been to encourage you to think about your child's needs and what your responsibilities are during their formative years. Of course, everyone hopes that you and your children will enjoy many happy times together as a family. But, alongside this is the knowledge that adoption is a life-long issue for adopted people, their birth parents and their adopters. For much of the time it may be in the background, but when it comes to the fore the foundation you have built during childhood will be the platform for your child's adult understanding. This is about avoiding looking for rosy pictures and forging a strong relationship which acknowledges the child's origins in a different family. Whatever your child's level of interest in this other family, it is in talking, listening and communicating with your particular child, especially during the pre-teen years, that you will deepen your understanding of his or her needs, learn how to respond and develop those lifetime relationships that are at the heart of building a family by adoption.

# Talking to children at different ages and stages: one family's experience

Right from the beginning we built up a loose-leaf album with special photographs – Peter as a tiny baby, one we fortunately had of Janet, his birth mother, visits to his foster home, his first day with us, special events together, the celebration tea we had when his adoption order was granted.

Sometimes when he was very young, cuddled up together after a bath looking at picture books, we would look at Peter's album mostly pointing out colours and naming things, but also each time talking of Janet as his "first" mum, saying he grew from a tiny egg in her tummy before he came to live with us and be adopted.

Of course we showed great pleasure in the photograph of the day he was adopted. When he was small each year we had a special cake at teatime on that date and grandma and grandpa joined us. We looked at the album again then. If we heard of someone who was adopted we might say, 'How nice, just like you'.

From about three, Peter really liked reading stories especially with lots of repetition. We added words to the photograph album – just very simply like – 'This is Peter, and here is Janet. Peter grew from a tiny egg in her tummy. Janet wanted Peter to be happy but she did not have a home for him. Peter went to stay with Auntie Sarah just for a little while. He was a very good baby but got lots of hiccups. Janet wanted Peter to have a new mummy and daddy who would love him and look after him. She heard about Anne and Derek (us!) and thought they sounded just right for Peter. Anne and Derek were so excited. They were so sad when they could not grow a baby themselves…now they could adopt Peter. Anne and Derek jumped into their blue car and went to Auntie Sarah's house to see Peter. He was wearing…'

I don't know how much he understood but we put in lots of sound effects and different voices for sad and excited and we read it lots of times. Sometimes he would want to read it every night for a week – then he would be on to something else. Sometimes he would ask questions, mostly simple factual things. Some we had to be careful about – like when he said he did not like Janet's hair and hoped he'd have hair like mine!

Other events could spark questions – like when a close family friend was pregnant and he wondered who would adopt her baby! Sorting that out led him to ask more about why Janet didn't keep him. As he was a bit older then, about six-and-a-half, we could tell him more about Janet's problems – like the fact that as a teenager she had lots of rows with her mum and step-dad and eventually she left home, but she had no job, she wouldn't ask them to help, and she stayed with various friends. She had a boyfriend called Jason who was Peter's first dad. We tried to emphasise that while Janet's life was in a bit of a mess when Peter was born, she did care about him and wanted the best for him. We explained that sometimes Janet didn't have enough money to buy his milk, or other times she was so tired she was frightened she would fall asleep and not hear him cry when it was time for his feed. Once he surprised us by wondering if Janet would know about his part in the school play – and then asking if we could tell her. We chose a nice photograph together and wrote about what he was doing (including the play!) and sent it all to our adoption agency for her if she should get in touch with them.

When we adopted our second child there was another burst of questions – particularly comparing first visits – like was he the same size as his new sister when we saw him first. There were more questions about why we could not have babies. He saw different people visiting and as we explained about the court, he checked out that once the judge decided, he really belonged in our family.

Once Peter was about eight or nine there seemed to be times when he worried more about Janet. Sometimes we would find him looking thoughtfully at her photograph. He would wonder what she was doing now. Obviously we could not answer but we told him more about what we knew. This included explaining that when she was unhappy she had started taking drugs as she hoped this would make things better but it didn't. He had already been asking us some questions about that with all the mention of drugs on the TV. Sometimes we would be able to talk easily together, at other times he would act as though he couldn't care less or tell us to shut up as he didn't want to talk about it.

Peter's school covers sex education at about age 10. This seemed to spark off questions about his first dad – and we knew very little about Jason. Again we tried writing to our adoption agency. They sent us a letter including all the information they had but I think Peter would have liked more.

The teenage years were full of the usual ups and downs and different moods. Occasionally we would have really good chats round the kitchen table. Sometimes talking about the common adolescent concerns – behaviour and pressure from the others at school (particularly when a couple of older boys were suspended for using drugs), sex and girl friends and later on, contraception – plus of course all the hopes and fears for the future of the sort of adult he would be, we wondered if being adopted made a big difference.

Sometimes during rows Peter would shout, 'You can't tell me what to do – you're not my real parents anyway'. The first time this happened we were stunned and really hurt and asked ourselves, 'What have we done wrong?' However, we soon realised that what Peter was really doing was asking, 'Who am I? Am I the product of Janet and Jason or of you two, or a mixture of both?' The next time this happened we just said, quite calmly, 'We're not your birth parents, we wish we were because we're proud of you and love you so much. But if you had been born to us we might have missed out because you wouldn't be the special person you are!'

A few times Peter actually made the connection with Janet or brought up questions about his adoption – who he would be like, what he might have inherited from her or Jason and how much he would be like us. At other times we were aware of the links and that we were in sensitive areas but didn't want to make a big issue of it. There were also, however, periods when he just did not want to talk with us and would be very offhand or spend all his time in his room.

It would of course have to be at one of these times when a letter arrived from our adoption agency out of the blue saying that Janet had contacted them. She was delighted with the earlier photographs of Peter and would be happy if he wanted to get in touch in the future – she now had her life more in order. It did not seem a good time to tell Peter – but if we didn't we could equally be in trouble with him for not letting him know. In the end we told him about the letter and he just shrugged it off and wouldn't say anything. We did write back to the adoption agency so Janet wouldn't be left wondering what happened.

We were all thrilled when, at the age of 18, Peter got a place at university. We all went out for a celebration dinner and over a cup of coffee afterwards he suddenly said he would like to let Janet know. He wrote a note the next day and a couple of weeks later a congratulations card came back from Janet via the adoption agency. Peter is clear that at the moment that is enough for him. He wants to concentrate on his life at university. He thinks they might exchange cards and bits of information and maybe meet sometime in the future.

# Useful organisations

## Adoption UK

46 The Green
South Bar Street
Banbury
Oxfordshire
OX16 9AB
Tel: 01295 752240
Fax: 01295 752241
www.adoptionuk.org

Adoption UK is an organisation for adoptive parents, their children and those hoping to adopt. There are over 140 volunteer co-ordinators located throughout the UK and most of these hold meetings where a wide variety of topics related to adoption, including telling, can be discussed and there is the opportunity to meet people in similar circumstances. Adoption UK members include many types of adoptive family, from those who have adopted healthy babies to those who have enlarged their family with one or more older or disabled children. People intending to adopt can also join, as one of the best ways of finding out what adopting involves is to talk to people who've already done it.

Local groups usually hold some family events such as summer picnics, Christmas parties, etc, where children can meet other adopted children. From a child's point of view, it's very comforting to have some friends who are adopted as it makes the whole thing seem more normal and less "different". Knowing other adoptive families with new children and babies arriving keeps the subject near the surface and discussable. Adoption UK publishes a journal, *Adoption Today*, full of fascinating experiences of adopters and adopted people. It's worth joining just to read this. They also provide a range of further information packs and leaflets on specific topics and have a Resource Bank through which adopters can share similar experiences, and the After Adoption Network, an informal link for adopters.

To find out about other locally based self-help/support groups for adoptive parents you can contact your adoption agency or local authority social services department or social work department.

## Supporting adults affected by adoption – NORCAP

112 Church Road
Wheatley
Oxfordshire
OX33 1LU
Tel: 01865 875000
Fax: 01865 875686
www.norcap.org.uk

NORCAP is a support group which offers the opportunity to talk to people who have had similar experiences. There are many "contact leaders" around the country. The services it provides are aimed at adults rather than children.

NORCAP aims to help and counsel:

- adopted people who are thinking of searching for their birth parents – it will suggest ideas and viewpoints to be considered before making a decision which will have far-reaching consequences;
- birth parents who either long for, or dread, a contact from the past – they can be put in touch with others in the same position;
- adoptive parents whose lives will be affected by any search their adopted children may start – it offers reassurance that they are only trying to find out more about themselves, and can

provide information on ways of answering their child's
questions.

NORCAP encourages the use of intermediaries in making any
contact. NORCAP also has a small group interested in the particular
needs of "foundlings". Members receive a newsletter three times
per year and can buy other publications.

## British Association for Adoption and Fostering (BAAF)

BAAF is a registered charity and professional association for all those
working in the child care field. BAAF's work includes: giving advice
and information to members of the public on aspects of adoption,
fostering and child care issues; publishing a wide range of books,
training packs and leaflets as well as a quarterly journal on
adoption, fostering and child care issues; providing training and
consultancy services to social workers and other professionals to
help them improve the quality of medical, legal and social work
services to children and families; giving evidence to government
committees on subjects concerning children and families;
responding to consultative documents on changes in legislation and
regulations affecting children in or at risk of coming into care; and
helping to find new families for children through *Be My Parent*.

More information about BAAF can be obtained from our offices
listed below.

**Head Office**
Saffron House
6–10 Kirby Street
London
EC1N 8TS
Tel: 020 7421 2600
Fax: 020 7421 2601
www.baaf.org.uk

## Southern England
Saffron House
6–10 Kirby Street
London
EC1N 8TS
Tel: 020 7421 2671
Fax: 020 7421 2669

## Central and Northern England
Unit 4
Pavilion Business Park
Royds Hall Road
Wortley
Leeds
LS12 6AJ
Tel: 0113 289 1101
Fax: 0113 289 1177

## BAAF Cymru
7 Cleeve House
Lambourne Crescent
Cardiff
CF14 5GP
Tel: 029 2076 1155
Fax: 029 2074 7934

## BAAF Scotland
40 Shandwick Place
Edinburgh
EH2 4RT
Tel: 0131 220 4749
Fax: 0131 226 3778

**BAAF Northern Ireland**
Botanic House
1–5 Botanic Avenue
Belfast
BT7 1JG
Tel: 028 9031 5494
Fax: 028 9031 4516

# Post and after adoption centres

There are many well established after adoption services which provide support for adoptive families, adopted people and birth parents whose children were adopted. Many of them offer counselling, preferably in person, but also on the telephone or by correspondence, for individuals and families. Some also organise events which focus on matters related to adoption, and provide the opportunity for people to meet in common interest groups. Some, like the Post-Adoption Centre in London, arrange a periodic programme of workshops to help parents explore some of the issues involved in communicating with children about adoption and to consider new ideas and approaches.

The Adoption and Children Act 2002 introduced a clear responsibility for local authorities in England and Wales to provide adoption support services and the right of adoptive families to ask for an assessment of their support needs. New placements should have an adoption support plan.

In Scotland, the statutory duty to have a post-adoption counselling service was introduced in the Children (Scotland) Act 1995. A number of councils provide this service wholly or partly through a voluntary agency.

In Northern Ireland, Article 3 of The Adoption (NI) Order 1987 mandates that each Board (now each Health and Social Care Trust) maintains a service for children who have been or may be adopted and persons who have adopted or may adopt a child. The services must include 'counselling for persons with problems relating to adoption'. Voluntary adoption agencies also provide these services.

The range of services available is growing and may vary across the UK. A growing number of local authority social services/work departments and voluntary adoption agencies provide adoption support services.

### Post-Adoption Centre
5 Torriano Mews
Torriano Avenue
London NW5 2RZ
Tel: 020 7284 0555
www.postadoptioncentre.org.uk

### ATRAP (Association of Transracially Adopted People)
C/o Racial Equality Foundation
Unit 35
Kings Exchange
Tileyard Road
London N7 9AH
Tel: 020 7619 6231
www.atrap.port5.com/html/home.html

### After Adoption
12–14 Chapel Street
Salford
Manchester M3 7NN
Tel: 0161 839 4930
www.afteradoption.org.uk

### After Adoption Yorkshire & Humberside
31 Moor Road
Leeds LS6 4BG
Advice line: 0113 230 2100
www.afteradoptionyorkshire.org.uk

## After Adoption Wales

7 Neville Street
Riverside
Cardiff CF11 6LP
Advice line: 0800 056 8578
www.afteradoption.org.uk

## Adoption Support

Suite A, 6th Floor
Albany House
Hurst Street
Birmingham B5 4BD
Tel: 0121 666 6334
http://myweb.tiscali.co.uk/adoptionsupport/index.html

## After Adoption Counselling

Birthlink
21 Castle Street
Edinburgh EH2 3DN
Tel: 0131 225 6441
www.birthlink.org.uk

## Barnardo's Scottish Adoption Advice Service

Suite 5/3, Skypark SP5
45 Finnieston Street
Glasgow G3 8JU
Tel: 0141 248 7530
www.barnardos.org.uk/saas.htm

## Scottish Adoption Association

161 Constitution Street
Edinburgh EH6 7DF
Tel: 0131 553 5060
www.scottishadoption.org

### The Church of Ireland Adoption Society
Church of Ireland House
61–67 Donegall Street
Belfast BT1 2QH
Tel: 028 9023 3885
www.cofiadopt.org.uk/

### Family Care Society
511 Ormeau Road
Belfast BT7 3GS
Tel: 028 9069 1133
www.family-care-society.org

### AdOPT – Northern Ireland
7 University Street
Belfast BT7 1FY
Tel: 028 9031 9500
www.adoptni.org.uk

## Other useful organisations

### Parentline Plus
520 Highgate Studios
53–79 Highgate Road
Kentish Town
London NW5 1TL
Tel: 020 7284 5500
www.parentlineplus.org.uk
Parentline Plus, incorporating the former National Stepfamily
Association, is a charity working for and with parents, and provides
a range of advice services, messageboards, regular parenting groups
and workshops.

**Intercountry Adoption Centre**
64–66 High Street
Barnet
Hertfordshire EN5 5SJ
Advice line: 0870 516 8742
Fax: 020 8440 5675
www.icacentre.org.uk
Provides consultation days, workshops, information and advice to all
those involved in or considering intercountry adoption both before and
after the adoption takes place. Advice is also available for intercountry
adopted adults. A range of country-specific information booklets can be
ordered or downloaded from the website.

# Useful books

BAAF publications are listed on our website at **www.baaf.org.uk** and can be purchased there or by phone on 020 7421 2604 or from our offices. BAAF also maintains an email contact list for updates and new publications: to subscribe to this please visit www.baaf.org.uk.

## Books for adopted children and young people

*Camis J,* **My Life and Me**, *BAAF, 2001*
This life story book includes space for drawings, photographs, documents and a record of thoughts and feelings at various stages in the child's life. It is designed to be completed by children, with help and support from appropriate adults; practice guidelines provide help for those undertaking direct work.

*Camis, J,* **We are Fostering**, *BAAF, 2003*
Based on the principles of life story work, this colourful, durable workbook will help prepare birth children of families who foster or adopt to welcome new arrivals into their homes and lives. Space is provided for drawings, photos and a record of thoughts and feelings.

**Children's guide series**, *BAAF*
This series of children's guides provides simple and easily understood explanations of adoption and various other subjects.

*Shah S,* **Adoption: What it is and what it means**, *BAAF, 2003*
Designed to appeal to children and hold their interest, this booklet provides a good introduction to adoption, the process and

procedures, with easy to understand definitions. Colourful, vividly illustrated and presented in accessible and jargon-free language.

### Argent H, **What is Contact?**, *BAAF, 2004*

This colourful children's guide includes simple explanations of what contact is, the different types, and what it will mean for them.

### Shah S and Argent H, **Life Story Work: What it is and what it means**, *BAAF, 2006*

A colourful children's guide for children who are embarking on life story work or are already doing it, with simple explanations of what is a complex activity.

### **My Story series**, *BAAF, 1997, 1998*

A unique series of books for use with children separated from their birth parents. The stories are simply told and attractively illustrated in full colour. Worksheets at the back of each workbook will help children to compare and contrast their own experiences with those of the characters in the story.

### **Living with a new family: Nadia and Rashid's story**

Nadia is ten and Rashid seven. When their father died some years ago, their birth mother, Pat, found it hard to look after them. So Nadia and Rashid went to live with Jenny, a foster carer, and then with their new parents, Ayesha and Azeez.

### **Belonging doesn't mean forgetting: Nathan's story**

Nathan is a four-year-old African-Caribbean boy and has just started school. His birth mum, Rose, found it hard to be a good mum and wanted someone else to look after him. Nathan went to live with foster carers Tom and Delores. And then with Marlene, her daughter Sophie, Grannie and Aunty Bea.

### Hoping for the best: Jack's story

Jack is an eight-year-old white boy. His birth mum, Maria, couldn't look after him because she was unhappy and unwell. Jack went to live with Peter and Sarah. At first he was happy but then started to feel sad and mixed up. Peter and Sarah did not think they could be the right mum and dad for him and Jack had to leave.

### Joining together: Jo's story

Tomorrow will be a big day for eight-year-old Joanne. She is going to court with her mum, stepfather and baby brother to be adopted. Jo knows that although Dave isn't her birth father he wants to help look after her for the rest of her life.

### Feeling safe: Tina's story

Tina wasn't safe at home and now lives with Molly who is her foster carer. Tina had to move after she told a teacher about how her Dad's touches made her feel bad. She is not sure whether she will ever be able to live with her family again but feels safe with her foster family.

*Foxon J,* **The Nutmeg Series**
**Nutmeg Gets Adopted, Nutmeg Gets Cross, Nutmeg Gets a Letter, Nutmeg Gets a Little Help, Nutmeg Gets into Trouble, and Nutmeg Gets a Little Sister**, *BAAF, 2001, 2002, 2003, 2004, 2006 and 2007*
This series of books for children about Nutmeg the squirrel and his adoptive family offer a practical way to explore and understand some of the situations and feelings that can be linked to adoption. Subjects covered include painful memories, feelings of anger and confusion, and contact issues.

*Foxon J,* **Spark Learns to Fly**, *BAAF, 2007*
An engaging illustrated book for children aged four to ten, looking at the difficult issue of domestic violence and what this might mean for the children involved.

*Kahn H,* **Tia's Wishes** and **Tyler's Wishes**, *BAAF, 2002 and 2003*
Tia's Wishes and Tyler's Wishes, designed for girls and boys
respectively, encourage children to voice their fantasies about
adoption and to come to terms with reality. These interactive books,
complete with a selection of accessories, should be regarded as an
integral part of life story work for children aged four to ten.


*Lidster A,* **Chester and Daisy Move On**, *BAAF, 1995*
A delightful picture book about two bear cubs who go to live with a
foster family and are then prepared to move to an adoptive family.
For use with four to ten-year-olds.


*Argent H,* **Josh and Jaz have Three Mums**, *BAAF, 2007*
An illustrated story for children aged four to ten looking at the
subject of lesbian adoption and, more generally, diversity in family
structures.


*Griffith J,* **Picnic in the Park**, *BAAF, 2007*
A picture book for young children which, through the story of a
birthday picnic in the park, looks at how families can come in all
shapes and sizes.


**My Life Story** *CD-ROM, Information Plus, 2003*
This CD Rom will guide worker and child through a range of life
story activities to assemble key information, process current
situations and consider what the future might hold. Music, sound
effects, colour animation and attractive graphics add to the appeal.


*Sparks K,* **Why Adoption?**, **BAAF**, *1995*
Experiences to share for teenagers and their adoptive parents –
adoption as seen from a young person's perspective.


*Bond M,* **The Paddington Books**, *Collins*
These books are well known to most children but remember that

Paddington has to get used to living in a family for the first time. He has brought with him from Peru his scrapbook, a photo of his Aunt Lucy, and little else. He settles down in his new home despite many traumatic experiences but often thinks back to his past.

McAfee A and Browne A, **The Visitors who Came to Stay**, *Walker Books, 2000*
Kate lives alone with her dad. Life changes when Mary and her son Sean become regular visitors. An unusual and amusing book with remarkable illustrations.

Miller K A, **Did My First Mother Love Me?**, *Morning Glory Press, 1994, USA*
A story for an adopted child with a special section for adoptive parents. In the story Moyan has a letter from her birth mother which she needs to read with her adoptive mother; she then wonders: did my first mother love me?

**My Story** and **Our Story**, *Donor Conception Network, 2002*
Not specifically on adoption but useful to look at when talking to children about assisted reproduction. These books cover the subjects of children conceived by donor insemination and egg donation into a variety of family situations.

Plumtree D, **Helping Children to Build Self-Esteem**, *Jessica Kingsley, 2001*
This book was produced for a range of people who work with young children to help them develop. A number of the activities are easily adaptable for use on an individual basis with adopted children.

Striker S and Kimmel E, **The Anti-Colouring Book**, *Scholastic, 1986*
This interactive book for children aged five to ten contains a wide range of suggestions to stretch a child's imagination. Each page

gives a hint of a picture and a sentence at the bottom to get started.

*Wilson J,* **The Story of Tracy Beaker**, *Yearling Books, 1992*
Tracy is ten years old. She lives in a Children's Home but would like a real home one day. Written as Tracy's diary, this is a lively humorous book which reveals a lot of what goes on in the minds of children separated from their parents. A second book starring Tracy Beaker, The Dare Game (Yearling Books, 2001), is also available.

Keep a note of books that your child may have found useful during preparation so that you can locate these again if needed.

**Letterbox Library** has a wide variety of titles for children, covering many different family structures and diversity issues – call 020 7503 4801 or visit www.letterboxlibrary.com.

The book reviews published in *Adoption & Fostering*, BAAF's quarterly journal, and *Adoption Today*, the bi-monthly magazine from Adoption UK, can also provide ideas of useful titles.

A range of books have been designed to help children put together information about themselves and their family, which can help build self-confidence. *The Anti-Colouring Book* and *Helping Children to Build Self-Esteem*, listed above, are good examples. Some need careful screening in advance if they contain assumptions about families which are difficult for your child.

## Novels for teenagers

*Ashley B,* **The Trouble with Donovan Croft**, *OUP, 2002*
This is a story about an African-Caribbean boy fostered in a white family. Donovan is unhappy he couldn't speak. This book is about trying to find out ways of reaching this very confused boy – and the relationship between Donovan and his white foster brother.

*Blackman M,* **Hacker***, Corgi, 1992*
At the beginning of this book Vicki, adopted as a baby, isn't exactly best pals with her brother who was born into the family! But when her adoptive father is arrested and accused of stealing over a million pounds from the bank, she is thrust into an adventure with her brother trying to prove her father's innocence. The ending not only solves the crime but it also establishes the relationship between Vicki and her brother and how she belongs in the family.

*Leach B,* **Anna Who?***, Attic Press, 1994, Eire*
Anna's adopted. When she was little her mother used to call her "our special daughter". But now Anna is 14 and she doesn't feel so special anymore. All Anna wants to do is to get away from her family and discover who she really is. But then something happens and Anna slowly begins to realise that she doesn't need to know where she came from to know who she is.

*Lowry L,* **Find a Stranger, Say Goodbye***, Viking Kestrel Books, 1995*
The story of an adopted girl's search for her birth mother. Everything is going well in her present family but she needs to know her background. She carries out her searching in a responsible way and the feelings it stirs up are realistic. Eventually she finds her birth mother and returns to her adoptive family who she discovers to be her "real" parents.

*Nerlove E,* **Who is David?***, Child Welfare League of America Inc, 1985, USA*
An involving story that should capture the attention of many adopted adolescents, especially boys. David struggles with his curiosity about his original parents in a happy adoptive home. His emerging friendship with Diana is sensitively described.

*Noel D,* **Five to Seven: The story of a 1920s childhood***, Robin Clark, 1991*
A small girl copes with the terrors of life caused by unpredictable adults, and separation from the key figure in her life.

*Paterson K,* **The Great Gilly Hopkins***, Harper Collins, 2004*
Gilly Hopkins is a tough operator – she's super cool and super intelligent. And she's not going to be had by anyone: teacher, social worker or foster parent. All she wants is a reunion with her beautiful long-lost mother. But just when it appears her dream might come true, things no longer seem quite so clear cut.

*Pearce P,* **The Way to Satin Shore***, Viking Kestrel, 1983*
Kate's family refuse to tell her about her dead father. They do not understand that until she finds out the truth about her father she cannot cope with living in the present.

Note: Children's books are regularly reviewed in *Adoption Today*, the newsletter published by Adoption UK (see Useful Organisations).

## Books for parents and carers

### Parenting

*Archer C,* **First Steps in Parenting the Child who Hurts***, Jessica Kingsley, 1999*
This book offers practical, sensitive guidance through the areas of separation, loss and trauma in early childhood. Archer sets out to encourage confidence, confessing this is the book she herself (as an adoptive parent) would have welcomed 20 years ago.

*Archer C,* **Next Steps in Parenting the Child who Hurts***, Jessica Kingsley, 1999*
This volume follows on from the First Steps book, continuing the challenging journey through childhood and into adolescence,

explaining the effects of early emotional trauma and reviewing specific sensitive situations that commonly arise.

*Argent H,* **Related by Adoption***, BAAF, 2004*
Grandparents and other relatives who become related by adoption can play an invaluable role in the life of the adopted child. This handbook gives an introduction to adoption today and discusses how the wider family can provide support.

*Cairns B,* **Fostering Attachments***, BAAF, 2004*
Brian Cairns draws on his considerable practical fostering experience to present a compelling insight into the challenges and rewards of foster family life. Full of practical ideas and useful suggestions for helping families to help themselves.

*Cairns K,* **Attachment, Trauma and Resilience***, BAAF, 2002*
One of BAAF's bestselling titles, this compelling book draws on the author's professional and personal experience of 25 years of fostering to explore how her family responded to the children's difficult feelings and behaviour. Suggestions for how to help promote recovery and develop resilience are woven throughout the story.

**Finding a Way Through***, (video), Kate Cairns in conversation with John Simmonds, BAAF, 2003*
John Simmonds, Director of Policy, Research and Development at BAAF, talks to Kate Cairns, author of Attachment, Trauma and Resilience, about her experiences of being a parent/carer on this 60 minute video, an essential supplement to Kate's highly regarded book.

*Hicks S and McDermott J,* **Lesbian and Gay Fostering and Adoption***, Jessica Kingsley, 1998*
This immensely readable book will be of enormous encouragement to lesbians or gay men who foster or adopt, or are considering

doing so. It tells openly and honestly how it is without becoming
weighted down with politics or jargon.

*Howe D,* **Adopters on Adoption**, *BAAF, 1996*
This absorbing collection of personal stories from experienced
adopters whose children are now young adults describes the
importance and distinctiveness of adoptive parenting. An essential
read for adopters and adoptive people.

*Lord J,* **Adopting a Child: A guide for people interested in
adoption**, *BAAF, 2002*
Essential reading for anyone who is considering adopting a child and
very useful for existing adoptive parents, this down-to-earth guide
gives clear and up-to-date information on all stages of the adoption
process. It includes names and addresses of adoption and fostering
agencies throughout the country, with maps showing their location,
and details of other organisations concerned with adoption.

**The Our Story Series**, *BAAF*
This series of real-life adoption memoirs, written by adopters, looks
at a variety of adoption scenarios and experiences.

*James M,* **An Adoption Diary**, *BAAF, 2006*
An inspiring real-life narrative of one couple's journey to adoptive
parenthood, which talks openly and honestly about the adoption
process.

*Seymour N,* **In Black and White**, *BAAF, 2007*
An honest account describing a white couple's adoption of two
black children, over a 20 year period. The story follows the children
through contact with their birth family and the effect this has on
their lives.

*Wise J,* **Flying Solo***, BAAF, 2007*
A humorous and heart-warming personal story which follows the author as she adopts a child on her own; this book describes the realities of life for single adopters.

*Mulholland J,* **Special and Odd***, BAAF, 2007*
A revealing and extraordinarily witty memoir which tells the story of how the author met his birth mother 29 years after being given up for adoption.

*Campbell N,* **Blue Eyed Son***, Pan Books, 2005*
An honest and revealing account of the author's journey to trace his birth family, and the impact this had upon his life.

*Morris A,* **The Adoption Experience***, Jessica Kingsley, 1999*
Actual adopters tell it like it is at every stage of the adoption process, from the moment of first deciding to adopt to feelings about children seeking a reunion with birth family members, or simply leaving home.

*Salter A,* **The Adopter's Handbook***, BAAF, 2006*
The first of its kind, this guide aims to help adopters help themselves through the adoption process and beyond. Information is included on processes, legal issues, education and health, needs of the child and parent, and post-adoption support.

*Van Gulden H and Bartels-Rabb L,* **Real Parents, Real Children***, Crossroads, 1995*
This book takes parents and professionals through the stages of child development, explaining what adopted children at each age commonly think and feel about adoption and how parents can respond.

## Adoption support

*Argent H,* **Models of Adoption Support***, BAAF, 2003*
This anthology gives a snapshot of what is happening in the area of
adoption support, from a variety of contributors who develop,
provide or use it; when and how often it is needed; how it can help;
and what is available and how to get it.

*Phillips R and McWilliam E,* **After Adoption: Working with
adoptive families***, BAAF, 1996*
This unique anthology, illustrated with case studies, focuses on post-
adoption support for adoptive families.

## Searching and reunion

*Feast J, Marwood M, Seabrooks S, Webb L,* **Preparing For
Reunion***, The Children's Society, 1998*
Adopted people, adoptive parents and birth parents tell their stories.
This book addresses many of the commonly asked questions like,
when should I search? What am I letting myself in for? Am I being
disloyal? Should I keep this secret? Do I really need counselling?

*Feast J and Philpot T,* **Searching Questions***, BAAF, 2003*
This book and accompanying video, based on a unique study,
highlight the issues involved in searching for birth relatives and
provide a greater understanding of the complexities and feelings
which may be involved.

*Howe D and Feast J,* **Adoption, Search and Reunion***, BAAF, 2004*
This fascinating study compares a group of adopted people who
searched for birth relatives with a group who did not, looking in
detail at the factors that influenced their decisions. The extensive
quotes from adopted people provide an absorbing read.

*Triseliotis J, Feast J and Kyle F,* **The Adoption Triangle Revisited***, BAAF, 2005*
This book presents the findings of a groundbreaking study which tracked the adoption and reunion experiences of adoptive parents, birth mothers and fathers, and adopted people. Includes fascinating insights for all those interested in searching and reunion.

*Mullender A and Kearn S,* **I'm Here Waiting: Birth relatives' views on Part II of the Adoption Contact Register for England and Wales***, BAAF, 1997*
This study explores the views of birth relatives on the Register and highlights the anomalies created by current legislation.

## Useful guides

*Barn R,* **Working with Black Children and Adolescents in Need***, BAAF, 1999*
This book aims to help develop an overall understanding of "race" and culture. Themes tackled include strengthening racial identity, developing anti-discriminatory practice and meeting the needs of transracially adopted black children.

*Douglas A and Philpot T,* **Adoption: Changing families, changing times***, Routledge, 2002*
Drawing together contributions from adopted people, birth parents, adoptive parents and practitioners, this anthology provides unique insights into the subject of adoption and exposes some of the myths surrounding it.

*Gilligan R,* **Promoting Resilience***, BAAF, (forthcoming) 2008*
This book is packed with practical ideas on how to improve children's quality of life by using relationship opportunities in their family, social and school networks, informed by the concept of resilience.

*Keefer B and Schooler J,* **Telling the Truth to your Adopted or Foster Child**, *Greenwood, 2000*
A collection of practical guidelines and tools to help parents communicate with their children about the circumstances of their past.

*Nicholls E,* **The New Life Work Model**, *Russell House, 2005*
A practice guide looking at how to make life story work more effective, and broadening its focus from immediate to lifelong needs.

*Ryan T and Walker R,* **Life Story Work**, *BAAF, 2007*
An invaluable guide to the innovative and imaginative techniques now available to help children come to terms with their painful pasts. It outlines the background theory and offers practical suggestions for using games and projects like family trees, maps and life graphs that aid the healing process.

## Adopted children

*Thomas C and Beckford B,* **Adopted Children Speaking**, *BAAF, 1999*
A book of poignant testimonies offering revealing insights into what children and young people think about adoption. Themes covered include beginning the process; matching and introductions; contact; and adoptive home and school.

## Contact

*Argent H,* **Staying Connected**, *BAAF, 2002*
Making and managing contact arrangements can be complex and challenging. This anthology offers varied practice examples to explore what works and what does not. Contributions come from both childcare practitioners and adopted people and their families.

*Neil E and Howe D,* **Contact in Adoption and Permanent Foster Care**, *BAAF, 2004*
This book gathers together the latest thoughts and research findings on the subject of contact in adoption and permanent foster care, looking at both infant and older child placements.

*Bond H,* **Ten Top Tips in Managing Contact**, *BAAF, 2007*
A handy guide to some fundamental positive steps that social workers, parents and carers can take to ensure that contact is a beneficial experience for all.

## Other books

**Surviving Five**, *Barnardo's, 1993*
This short, very readable book gives an insight into how one family coped with the different needs of a family of five brothers and sisters from introductions through the first year of placement, looking at issues to be addressed with children at different ages.

*Bernstein A C,* **Flight of the Stork: What children think (and when) about sex and family building**, *Perspectives Press, 1994*
An expansion of an earlier book on talking to children about sex, recognising their needs and what they understand at different stages of development. The new edition includes chapters on children born as a result of assisted reproduction and those growing up in adoptive and stepfamilies.

*Charlton L, Crank M, Kansara K, Oliver C,* **Still Screaming: Birth parents compulsorily separated from their children**, *After Adoption, 1998*
Provides revealing and hard-hitting accounts of what birth parents think and feel when their children are adopted against their wishes.

*Howe D, Sawbridge P, Hinings D,* **Half a Million Women***, The Post-Adoption Centre, 1997*
Examines aspects of the experience of giving up a child for adoption.

*Jones M,* **Everything you Need to Know about Adoption***, Sheldon House (SPCK), 1987*
A very useful guide to adoption with plenty of quotations from people who've "done it". Includes material on transracial and intercountry adoption.

*Kay J,* **The Adoption Papers***, Bloodaxe Books, 1991*
Jackie Kay was adopted transracially by a white Scottish couple. This collection of poetry expresses the different viewpoints of the mother, birth mother, and daughter.

*Harris P (ed),* **In Search of Belonging***, BAAF, 2006*
An anthology of writings, memoirs, poetry and artwork by transracially adopted people from countries as different as Kenya, Hong Kong, Cambodia and Sri Lanka.

*Bishoff T and Rankin J (eds),* **Seeds from a Silent Tree***, Pandal Press, 1997*
An anthology of thoughts, writings and memoirs by transracially adopted people from Korea, looking at their experiences of adoption and feelings about their identity.

*Krementz J,* **How it Feels to be Adopted***, Orion, 1984*
The views of 19 adopted young people in the USA, ranging in age from 8 to 16 years old. It could be read by adults or children and reflects many of the feelings children have about their adoption.

*Post-Adoption Centre,* **A Glimpse through the Looking Glass***, 1990*
A discussion paper that examines issues of relevance to transracially adopted black adults.

*Rosenberg E B,* **The Adoption Life Cycle***, The Free Press, 1992*
A readable book which combines current research theory and practical advice relevant to all those directly involved in the adoption experience – adopters, adoptive parents and birth parents, as well as professionals. It provides a framework for understanding the important developmental tasks which span the lifetimes of those involved.

*Ruskai Melina L,* **Making Sense of Adoption***, Harper & Row, 1989*
This book includes advice and many examples of age-specific activities to help answer questions like - How do I share information that might upset my child? How can I know when my child is wondering about adoption?

*Tugendhat J,* **The Adoption Triangle***, Bloomsbury, 1992*
What happens when adopted people wish to search for their lost families? This book includes interviews with many adopted adults, birth parents, and adoptive parents and those professionally involved. Starting from looking at the particular perspectives of birth mother, birth father, adopted individual and adoptive parents, it goes on to explore both the search and reunions.

*Verrier N,* **The Primal Wound***, Gateway, 1996*
This is an in-depth exploration of pre- and perinatal psychology, attachment, bonding and loss, and explores the effects on adopted children of separation from the birth mother.

*Wells S,* **Within me, Without me***, Scarlet Press, 1994*
This collection of personal stories explores the experiences of mothers who have given up children for adoption.

**Note:** Books for adults are regularly reviewed in *Adoption & Fostering*, BAAF's journal and in *Adoption Today*, the newsletter published by Adoption UK (see Useful Organisations for details).

# Leaflets from BAAF – Advice Note series

### Adoption: Some questions answered
Basic information about adoption – the processes, procedures, the law and useful resources.

### If you are Adopted
Answers to some of the questions adopted children ask, aimed at the children themselves. Includes information on tracing birth parents.

### Intercountry Adoption: Information and guidance
Information on adopting a child from overseas, including procedures, legislation, and where to obtain advice and further information.

### Stepchildren and Adoption (separate editions for England & Wales and Scotland)
Information on stepfamilies, the advantages or not of adoption, the alternatives and obtaining further advice.

### Talking about Origins
An outline of adopted children's need to be told about adoption and the law on access to birth certificates and information.

### For further reading
Articles regularly appear in BAAF's quarterly journal, Adoption & Fostering, which may be of interest to adoptive parents. For subscription details, contact BAAF or visit www.baaf.org.uk.

# The Our Story series

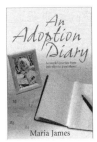

Maria James

Nathalie Seymour

Julia Wise

Karen Carr

### An Adoption Diary
This is a true story of an adoption - a story that follows Maria's and Rob's adoption of a two-year-old child, spanning a period of four years and chronicling the highs and lows along the way.

### In Black and White
This book tells how Tom and Nathalie, a white couple, established a transracial family by adopting the two children of a young black woman. Spanning some thirty years from the children's adoption to the present, this honest account looks at the dramatic events which followed.

### Flying Solo
In this heartwarming and humorous account, Julia Wise tells of how she gave up a high-flying career to adopt a child on her own. Inspiring and accessible, this book describes the realities of life as a single adoptive parent.

### Adoption Undone
This is the true story of an adoption and an adoption breakdown, bravely told by the adoptive mother. From the final court hearing, when Lucy returned to local authority care, Karen Carr looks back over four years and describes what went wrong and why.